The Best Way To Better Golf

Jack Nicklaus

CORONET BOOKS
Hodder and Stoughton

First published by Fawcett Publications, Inc.,
New York

Coronet edition 1968
Nineteenth impression 1986

Printed and bound in Great Britain for
Hodder and Stoughton Paperbacks, a
division of Hodder and Stoughton Ltd,
Mill Road, Dunton Green, Sevenoaks,
Kent (Editorial office: 47 Bedford
Square, London WC1 3DP) by
Richard Clay (The Chaucer Press) Ltd,
Bungay, Suffolk

ISBN 0 340 04348 2

CONTENTS

Introduction

They say that golf is a game of imitation. That's one reason why children make the best golf pupils. They are natural mimics who don't start out with any previous misconceptions about the game built up in their minds. Unfortunately, most adults do, and often the first lesson is to erase their false illusions.

What I hope to achieve in this book is to create a mirror into which you can look and see yourself playing better golf. I also want to simplify the process, because golf already has become too complicated for the learning player. And it is, after all, a game. I believe the best and easiest way for me to communicate my ideas to you is through the clear and simple illustrations that appear on these pages.

Learning from watching others has proved to be a successful method of golf instruction in recent years, although it has taken many forms. Today, you can study stop-action photographs in golf magazines, take tips from your favorite professionals on television, or analyze line drawings like the ones in this book. But they all have the same basic idea: to implant in your mind the correct way to execute a given golf problem. Once you have a clear picture of it trapped in your brain, you can, within the bounds of your own physical capacities, duplicate it.

In preparing this book, I have divided it into sections in a way I think will be most beneficial to the average week-end golfer. I'm talking about the fellow who is trying to get down into the 90's or 80's. Some of the tips here may seem a little too basic or repetitious to the more advanced golfer, but I have found that the only way to play better golf is by repetition. Frequently on the pro tour, I will find that I'm not scoring as well as I think I should. When I go out to the practice tee to work it out, more often than not I'll discover my trouble was caused by a little slip-up in the basics. Maybe I was getting a little careless about my grip, or possibly I wasn't lining up properly for my shots. Even pros can be guilty of these goofs, and only by going back to the fundamentals do we get back on the right track.

The same logic applies to the recreational golfer—only more so. Because he doesn't play the game under the same day-to-day conditions that we do, he is more prone to errors, and his game suffers. The high-handicapper, obviously, doesn't get to play more than once or twice a week, and in between rounds he is very likely to experience a breakdown in some part of his game. The best way to use this book is to keep a club in your hand while reading it. With the book at your side, you can try out some of the pointers that cover a particular problem of yours. Such things as gripping a club, putting, or even chip shots can be accomplished right in your own living room. This will give you a feel of things while you're reading, and among other things I've mentioned, golf is a game of feel. You feel your shots in much the same manner a blind man reads through braille.

While I don't intend for this book to serve as a substitute for the golf instruction you get from a professional, I do believe it will help you achieve a more consistent game. In other words, I hope to supplement the sound golf principles you already have absorbed. Above all, I hope that through this book you will find the way to improve your game, for, as I have found out, the better I play golf, the more I enjoy it.

Jack Nicklaus

CHAPTER 1

The Basics

No matter what you may accomplish in golf, regardless of how sophisticated your game may become, it will always rise and fall on your ability to master the fundamentals. Relax your grip even slightly, grow the least bit careless on the takeaway of your backswing, and your game will collapse on you like a house of cards. There is no substitute for correctness, and this is why I stress the basics so strongly whenever I give golf clinics.

It all starts with the hands, or more specifically, the grip. It doesn't matter which of the three generally accepted grips you choose—interlocking, overlapping or full-finger (baseball)—the grip is the key to a sound swing and successful scoring. After studying and trying out the grips illustrated in this section, settle on the one you and your professional agree suits you the best and then stick with it.

Keeping the proper distance from the ball at address is another primer that golfers of all handicaps often overlook. The smoothest swing in the world will be squandered by not positioning yourself correctly with the ball. Use these reminders to avoid falling into a bad—and costly—habit: stand upright with shoulders natural; flex your knees slightly and let your shoulders now slump forward but relaxed; grip your club and extend it directly behind the ball. This places the arms in much the same position they will be in at impact and allows you to swing freely around your body without reaching or bending backward.

Once you have fully grasped the meaning of grip and stance, you are then ready to tackle the other basics that make up this chapter and upon which your whole golf game is built.

The GRIP

It is both appropriate and compulsory to begin here with the *GRIP*— for the grip is the very *BEGINNING* of the swing.

Without a natural and correct union of the hands and club, it is impossible to transmit *MAXIMUM CONTROL* to the stroke.

Pictured are the three types of grips generally used today—they are basically alike except in the *LINKAGE*. Because of my small hands, I use the *INTERLOCKING*. This grip feels natural to me and allows my hands to work more as a unit. Find which grip best suits *YOUR* type of hands.

• *THE INTERLOCKING* •
INDEX FINGER OF LEFT HAND IS INTERTWINED WITH LITTLE FINGER OF RIGHT HAND—

• *THE OVERLAPPING* •
LITTLE FINGER OF RIGHT HAND IS PLACED OVER LEFT HAND BETWEEN INDEX AND MIDDLE FINGERS.

• *THE BASEBALL* •
ALL TEN FINGERS ARE PLACED DIRECTLY ON THE CLUB.

•KEEP A FIRM GRIP•

ONE OF THE MAJOR DEMANDS OF CONSISTENT GOLF IS TO MAINTAIN A CONSTANT PRESSURE ON THE GRIP THROUGHOUT THE SWING, EVEN *AFTER* THE BALL IS STRUCK...

BARRETT TAYLOR

...ALLOWING THE HANDS TO LOOSEN JUST AFTER IMPACT MAY NOT RESULT IN LOSS OF CLUBHEAD SPEED, BUT IT WILL CAUSE A LOSS OF FIRMNESS AND CONTROL TO THE SHOT.

• LINING UP •

ALIGNMENT IS ONE THE MOST VITAL ASPECTS OF WINNING FORM. PROPERLY ALIGNED, EVEN A MEDIOCRE SWINGER CAN HIT THE BALL REASONABLY WELL; BUT THE GREATEST SWING IN THE WORLD WON'T HELP IF YOUR AIM IS WRONG.

ON THE PRACTICE TEE, A CLUB PLACED ON THE GROUND WILL HELP...

...HOWEVER, SINCE THIS IS ILLEGAL IN ACTUAL PLAY, HERE'S WHAT I SOMETIMES DO.

FIRST, I STUDY THE LINE FROM BEHIND THE BALL. THEN STANDING THUS, I LAY THE CLUB IN BACK OF THE BALL, SQUARE WITH THE TARGET. FINALLY, WITHOUT CHANGING CLUBHEAD POSITION, I WALK AROUND THE BALL UNTIL I AM IN THE CORRECT ADDRESS POSITION.

A GAP IN YOUR GRIP CAN PUT A GAP IN YOUR GAME

A GREAT NUMBER OF GOLFERS ARE QUITE AWARE THAT THEIR HANDS LOOSEN ON THE GRIP AT THE TOP OF THE SWING, BUT TAKE NO CORRECTIVE ACTION, FEELING THAT BY REGRIPPING ON THE DOWNSWING THEY WILL ARRIVE AT THE BALL NO WORSE FOR WEAR.

THEY FAIL TO REALIZE THAT THE PROCESS OF LOOSENING THEN REFIRMING THE GRIP CHANGES THE POSITION OF THE CLUBFACE, CAUSING IT TO MEET THE BALL AT AN INCORRECT ANGLE.

SOLID, ACCURATE SHOTS REQUIRE THAT THE CLUBFACE REMAINS SQUARE FROM ADDRESS TO IMPACT. THIS CANNOT BE ACHIEVED WITHOUT A FIRM UNCHANGING GRIP.

GRIP FIRM AT TOP

It is extremely important that the grip be *FIRM* at the top of the backswing.

The club should be held firmly throughout the swing, particularly at the critical juncture between the backswing and the downswing.

When you *LOOSEN* your hands at the top, you've lost control of the swing. You'll change your entire plane— your entire rhythm; you'll change a little bit of everything.

However, don't squeeze the club as though you were choking a snake. The hands should be firm, but passive.

• KEEP GRIP NATURAL •

ONE IMPORTANT FEATURE OF CORRECT GRIPPING IS BEING ABLE TO RETURN THE CLUBFACE TO THE BALL IN A NATURAL WAY.

THUS, THE GRIP ITSELF MUST BE NATURAL AT THE **START**. THIS ENTAILS PLACING THE HANDS SO THAT THE **PALM** OF THE **RIGHT** HAND, THE **BACK** OF THE **LEFT** HAND AND THE CLUBFACE ARE ALL **SQUARE** TO THE TARGET. THIS ALSO IS THE CORRECT **IMPACT** POSITION.

START WITH A SOUND GRIP AND YOU WILL END RIGHT, PROVIDED THE REST OF THE SWING IS CORRECT.

STANCE

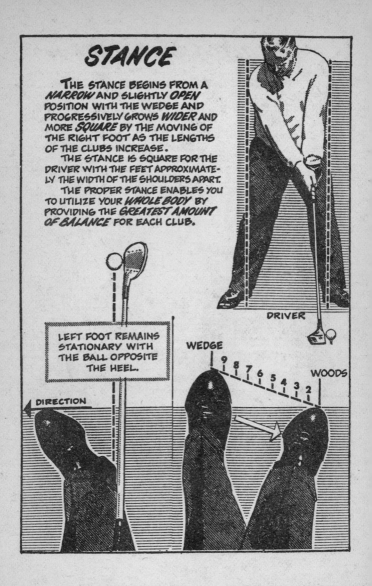

THE STANCE BEGINS FROM A *NARROW* AND SLIGHTLY *OPEN* POSITION WITH THE WEDGE AND PROGRESSIVELY GROWS *WIDER* AND MORE *SQUARE* BY THE MOVING OF THE RIGHT FOOT AS THE LENGTHS OF THE CLUBS INCREASE.

THE STANCE IS SQUARE FOR THE DRIVER WITH THE FEET APPROXIMATELY THE WIDTH OF THE SHOULDERS APART.

THE PROPER STANCE ENABLES YOU TO UTILIZE YOUR *WHOLE BODY* BY PROVIDING THE *GREATEST AMOUNT OF BALANCE* FOR EACH CLUB.

DRIVER

LEFT FOOT REMAINS STATIONARY WITH THE BALL OPPOSITE THE HEEL.

WEDGE

9 8 7 6 5 4 3 2

WOODS

DIRECTION

AVOID TOO WIDE A STANCE

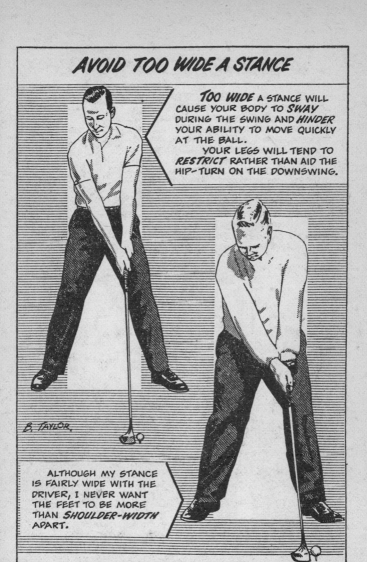

TOO WIDE A STANCE WILL CAUSE YOUR BODY TO **SWAY** DURING THE SWING AND **HINDER** YOUR ABILITY TO MOVE QUICKLY AT THE BALL.

YOUR LEGS WILL TEND TO **RESTRICT** RATHER THAN AID THE HIP-TURN ON THE DOWNSWING.

B. TAYLOR

ALTHOUGH MY STANCE IS FAIRLY WIDE WITH THE DRIVER, I NEVER WANT THE FEET TO BE MORE THAN **SHOULDER-WIDTH** APART.

IMPORTANCE of BALL POSITION

AS BRIEFLY DESCRIBED PREVIOUSLY, THE POSITION OF THE BALL FOR NORMAL SHOTS IS ON A LINE OPPOSITE THE *LEFT HEEL* — THIS IS THE ONLY PLACE IN THE SWING'S ARC WHERE THE CLUB STRAIGHTENS OUT ONTO A LINE *PARALLEL* TO THE DIRECTION OF THE TARGET.

A BALL POSITIONED BACK TOWARD THE RIGHT FOOT WILL GO TO THE *RIGHT* WHEN STRUCK BECAUSE THE CLUB IS STILL TRAVELING FROM THE *INSIDE-OUT.*

A BALL POSITIONED *BEYOND* THE LEFT HEEL WILL BE STRUCK AFTER THE CLUB HAS STARTED AROUND TO THE *LEFT* — THEREFORE THE BALL WILL GO LEFT.

PLAY THE BALL OFF THE LEFT HEEL FOR *ALL* CLUBS — RIGHT FOOT IS DRAWN BACK TO FORM A WIDER AND MORE SQUARE STANCE AS CLUB LENGTH INCREASES.

DRIVER   WEDGE

• KEEP A LEVEL HEAD •

AS I HAVE PREVIOUSLY STATED, *HEAD POSITION* IS THE MOST IMPORTANT THING IN GOLF. THE POINT I'D LIKE TO STRESS TODAY IS THAT WHILE THE HEAD MUST NOT MOVE BACK OR FORTH, NEITHER MUST IT MOVE *UP* OR *DOWN*. BOBBING THE HEAD DISRUPTS THE WHOLE SWING AND MAKES CONTROL ALMOST IMPOSSIBLE.

BE ESPECIALLY CAREFUL NOT TO DROP YOUR HEAD ON THE BACKSWING, THEN KEEP IT ON THE SAME PLANE UNTIL WELL AFTER IMPACT. *REMEMBER,* A LEVEL HEAD MEANS A LEVEL BODY, A LEVEL SWING AND SOLID CONTACT.

SHOULDER ACTION

PROPER SHOULDER ACTION IS VITAL TO A FLUID, CONSISTENT SWING. SHOWN HERE ARE THREE WAYS IN WHICH THE SHOULDERS CAN TURN. I RECOMMEND ONLY ONE.

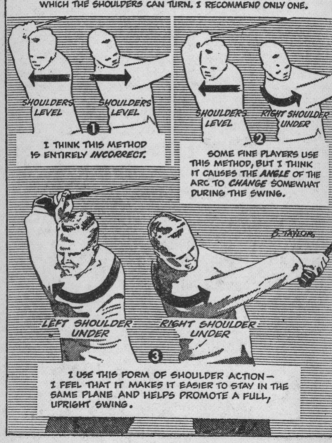

SHOULDERS LEVEL   SHOULDERS LEVEL   ①

I THINK THIS METHOD IS ENTIRELY *INCORRECT.*

SHOULDERS LEVEL   RIGHT SHOULDER UNDER   ②

SOME FINE PLAYERS USE THIS METHOD, BUT I THINK IT CAUSES THE *ANGLE* OF THE ARC TO *CHANGE* SOMEWHAT DURING THE SWING.

B. TAYLOR

LEFT SHOULDER UNDER   RIGHT SHOULDER UNDER   ③

I USE THIS FORM OF SHOULDER ACTION — I FEEL THAT IT MAKES IT EASIER TO STAY IN THE SAME PLANE AND HELPS PROMOTE A FULL, UPRIGHT SWING.

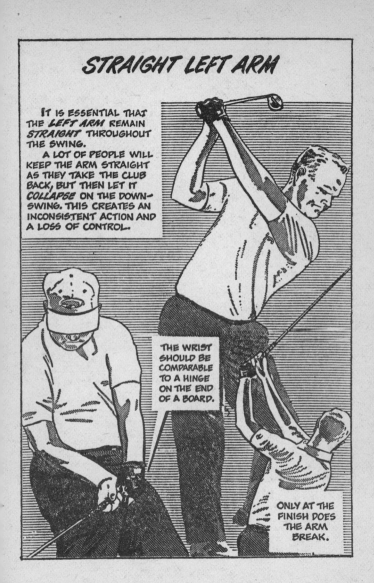

STRAIGHT LEFT ARM

IT IS ESSENTIAL THAT THE *LEFT ARM* REMAIN *STRAIGHT* THROUGHOUT THE SWING.

A LOT OF PEOPLE WILL KEEP THE ARM STRAIGHT AS THEY TAKE THE CLUB BACK, BUT THEN LET IT *COLLAPSE* ON THE DOWN-SWING. THIS CREATES AN INCONSISTENT ACTION AND A LOSS OF CONTROL.

THE WRIST SHOULD BE COMPARABLE TO A HINGE ON THE END OF A BOARD.

ONLY AT THE FINISH DOES THE ARM BREAK.

• ELBOW POSITION •

CONTRARY TO MANY EXISTING THEORIES AS TO HOW THE ELBOWS SHOULD POINT AT ADDRESS – SUCH AS, *DOWN, IN, OUT, OPPOSED, ETC.,* – GOLF SHOULD BE *NATURAL*, AND THE ELBOWS NEVER CONSCIOUSLY TURNED OR TWISTED.

BARRETT TAYLOR

AS YOU GRIP THE CLUB, YOUR ELBOWS SHOULD BE IN THE SAME POSITION AS WHEN THE ARMS HANG *NORMALLY* AT YOUR SIDES.

• The HIP-TURN •

THE ACTION OF THE HIPS DURING THE SWING CAN BE COMPARED TO A REVOLVING CYLINDER...

...ON THE BACKSWING THE RIGHT HIP TURNS UNTIL THE LEFT HIP AND SHOULDER BECOME EVEN WITH OR BEHIND THE BALL. THIS COILS THE BODY AND STORES UP POWER TO BE RELEASED ON THE DOWNSWING.

...EMPHASIS SHOULD BE PLACED ON TURNING THE RIGHT HIP BACK TOWARD THE BALL AND THE HOLE.

IF THE RIGHT HIP IS ROTATING PROPERLY THE REST OF THE BODY WILL FOLLOW IN PROPER SEQUENCE ALMOST AUTOMATICALLY.

ROLL the FEET

WHEN I FIRST BEGAN TO PLAY GOLF, I WAS TAUGHT THE *ROLLING FOOT ACTION*, AND I THINK THIS IS THE CORRECT METHOD IN ATTAINING PROPER FOOTWORK.

I WAS TAUGHT NEVER TO ALLOW THE HEEL OF EITHER FOOT TO LEAVE THE GROUND—

B. TAYLOR

ON THE BACKSWING I WOULD *ROLL* THE LEFT FOOT AND PLACE THE WEIGHT ON THE INSIDE OF THE RIGHT FOOT.

GOING THROUGH THE BALL I WOULD KEEP THE WEIGHT ON THE LEFT FOOT AND *ROLL* TO THE INSIDE OF THE RIGHT FOOT.

THIS SYSTEM ELIMINATES BODY SWAY AND KEEPS THE HEAD FROM MOVING. THE BODY IS HELD IN A STABLE POSITION BY A FIRM GRASP ON THE GROUND. THE RESULT IS *GOOD BALANCE*.

AS THE PLAYER BECOMES MORE PROFICIENT THROUGH EXPERIENCE, HE CAN ALLOW THE RIGHT FOOT TO LIFT SLIGHTLY ON THE FOLLOW-THROUGH. THE LEFT HEEL CAN ALSO LIFT SLIGHTLY ON THE BACKSWING WITH THE LONGER CLUBS.

WITH THE WEDGE, AS DESCRIBED BEFORE, THE LEFT FOOT *NEVER* ROLLS OR LIFTS.

POINT AT THE TARGET

AT THE TOP OF THE BACKSWING YOUR CLUBSHAFT SHOULD POINT IN A STRAIGHT-LINE DIRECTION TOWARD THE TARGET, WHETHER YOU TAKE THE CLUB TO PARALLEL OR, AS I DO, SHORT OF PARALLEL...

...THE PURPOSE IS TO MAINTAIN A RECIPROCATING STRAIGHT-LINE MOTION TO THE ARC THROUGHOUT THE SWING...

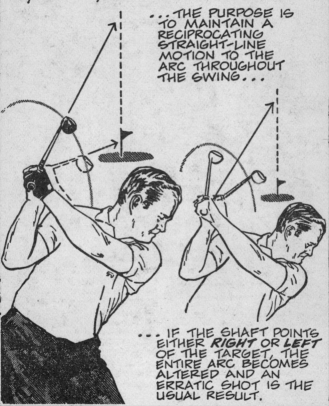

...IF THE SHAFT POINTS EITHER *RIGHT* OR *LEFT* OF THE TARGET, THE ENTIRE ARC BECOMES ALTERED AND AN ERRATIC SHOT IS THE USUAL RESULT.

WEIGHT DISTRIBUTION at ADDRESS

TO PROVIDE THE MOST NATURAL AND COMFORTABLE POSITION AT ADDRESS, THE WEIGHT MUST BE *EQUALLY* DIVIDED BETWEEN BOTH FEET.

ALSO HIGHLY IMPORTANT, THE PRESSURE MUST BE ON THE *INSIDE* OF THE FEET — FOR THIS IS, BASICALLY, WHERE IT REMAINS THROUGHOUT THE SWING.

WEIGHT IS NEITHER FORWARD NOR BACK, BUT EVENLY DIVIDED BETWEEN THE *BALL* AND *HEEL* OF EACH FOOT.

WEIGHT DISTRIBUTION *at the* TOP

BARRETT TAYLOR

FROM ADDRESS TO THE PEAK OF THE BACKSWING, THE WEIGHT IS HELD, BASICALLY, ON THE *INSIDE* OF THE FEET.

AT THE TOP 85 TO 90% OF THE WEIGHT HAS SHIFTED TO THE *INSIDE* OF THE *RIGHT* FOOT, THE REMAINDER STILL CARRIED BY THE INSIDE OF THE LEFT. THUS, THE BODY REMAINS CENTERED AND HIP TURN IS PERFORMED WITHOUT SWAY.

WEIGHT DISTRIBUTION DOWN and THROUGH

AS THE WEIGHT SHIFTS LEFT ON THE DOWNSWING PRESSURE REMAINS INSIDE BOTH FEET. JUST BEFORE IMPACT YOU SHOULD FEEL THAT THE **MAJORITY** OF THE WEIGHT IS ON THE **LEFT** FOOT.

NOT UNTIL YOU ARE **TWO** FEET THROUGH THE BALL SHOULD THE WEIGHT GO FROM THE INSIDE TO THE OUTSIDE OF THE LEFT FOOT. THE PLAYER WHO SHIFTS TO THE OUTSIDE TOO SOON WILL MOVE OUT BEYOND THE BALL.

AT THE FINISH 95% OF YOUR WEIGHT SHOULD BE ON THE LEFT FOOT

• SWING, DON'T STEER •

Unfortunately, the pressure of playing tight courses will cause many golfers to fall into the habit of trying to *steer* the ball instead of swinging freely...

BARRETT TAYLOR

...To derive the most from the game you must utilize the sum of your natural ability, and this cannot be done with a fearful jab at the ball.

Breaking the steering habit may take time, but you will perform much better in the clutch once you can consistently deliver a full free swing without undue concern over the outcome.

HIT THE BALL!

IN ADDITION TO THE BASIC REQUIREMENTS OF A SOUND GOLF SWING, SUCH AS TIMING, RHYTHM, BALANCE, ETC., THERE IS ANOTHER PRINCIPLE REQUIREMENT THAT MUST BE CONSIDERED BEFORE A PLAYER CAN ATTAIN MORE THAN PARTIAL SUCCESS — THE REQUIREMENT TO *HIT* THE BALL.

THIS MAY SEEM LIKE AN OBVIOUS FACT, BUT MANY A GOLFER THINKS TOO MUCH ABOUT *SWINGING* AND NOT ENOUGH ABOUT *HITTING*. IT'S ALWAYS NICE TO HAVE A SMOOTH, PRETTY SWING, BUT IF YOU DON'T CENTER YOUR CONCENTRATION UPON THE ACTUAL HITTING OF THE BALL, THEN YOU FAIL TO UTILIZE A GOOD SWING AND WASTE THE EFFORT YOU HAVE EXTENDED IN ACQUIRING GOOD FORM.

PRACTICE WITH TWO THINGS IN MIND. FIRST, A GOOD, SMOOTH SWING IS ESSENTIAL, BUT REMEMBER — THERE MUST BE A *HIT* APPLIED TO THE BALL.

BALANCE

I HAVE WRITTEN ABOUT THE IMPORTANCE OF *TIMING* AND *RHYTHM* IN THE GOLF SWING — *BALANCE* IS RIGHT IN THERE WITH THEM. IN FACT, BALANCE IS THE *RESULT* OF TIMING AND RHYTHM. IT IS DIFFICULT TO ATTAIN GOOD BALANCE IF THE SWING IS OUT OF TEMPO.

IN ORDER TO SHIFT THE WEIGHT PROPERLY, KEEP EVERYTHING IN THE CORRECT PLACE, AND REMAIN WELL BALANCED, YOU MUST SWING IN A SMOOTH FLOWING MANNER THAT NEITHER SLOWS NOR HURRIES THE ACTION. GOOD BALANCE BEGINS AT ADDRESS, CONTINUES THROUGH THE BACKSWING AND DOWNSWING AND REVEALS ITSELF AT THE FINISH. WHENEVER MY BALANCE IS OFF, I CHECK MY TIMING AND RHYTHM. I SUGGEST YOU DO THE SAME.

IF YOU'VE EVER WATCHED *SAM SNEAD* OR *BEN HOGAN* SWING, YOU'VE SEEN EXAMPLES OF MARVELOUS BALANCE — AND ITS REWARDS. I DOUBT IF EITHER PLAYER HAS EVER BEEN OFF-BALANCE IN OVER 30 YEARS OF TOURNAMENT GOLF.

TIMING ✚ RHYTHM ═ BALANCE

CHAPTER 2

The Swing

There are three basic parts to the golf swing—the backswing, downswing and follow-through—and in that cycle lies a multitude of terrors and errors which confronts all of us at one time or another. The swing is the sum of all its parts, but if we were to execute each part separately and consciously, there would be no rhythm to it and no buildup of power. And the purpose of the swing, after all, is to generate enough force to hit the ball a given distance.

The panels that appear in this chapter break down the swing into its various parts. By taking a club in your hands and practicing what you see in the illustrations, you will be able to work on each part of your swing and eventually meld them all together as a whole into what we call the one-piece swing. At first, each part of the swing must be thought out separately in practice, until it can be performed automatically; after a while, you won't have to think about it. Actually, in the two or three seconds it takes to complete a golf swing, your mind cannot possibly remember everything it has been taught. But the two things I do keep in mind when I'm swinging are to *take the club straight back as slowly as possible,* and *keep the head still.*

Ultimately, your swing will reflect your own golfing personality. This is far more desirable than singling out a favorite golfer and attempting to emulate his style. More harm than good can come from this, because the things that work for one golfer may not work for another due to personal differences in physical and mental makeup. It's best to develop your own swing in a fashion that harmonizes with your strength and build.

HANDS PROVIDE THE LINK

ONE GOOD POINT TO REMEMBER IN MAKING A PROPER BACKSWING IS THAT THE *HANDS* DO NOT ACTUATE THE TAKEAWAY, BUT SERVE ONLY TO HOLD THE CLUB...

...THE *LEFT ARM* AND *CLUBSHAFT* PERFORM AS A *ONE-PIECE UNIT*, WITH THE HANDS MERELY PROVIDING *LINKAGE* OF THE TWO...

BARRETT TAYLOR

...WITH THIS POINT IN MIND, THE BACKSWING BECOMES A SIMPLE MATTER OF THE BODY TURNING AROUND THE HEAD. THE HANDS WILL BREAK AUTOMATICALLY WHEN THE PROPER TIME ARRIVES.

START RIGHT TO END RIGHT

THE MOST VITAL PHASE OF THE GOLF SWING IS THE FIRST 15 INCHES OR SO OF THE TAKEAWAY FROM THE BALL.

PROBLEMS IN TIMING THE RELEASE THROUGH THE BALL CAN USUALLY BE TRACED BACK TO THE START OF THE BACKSWING.

A GOOD BACKSWING ALWAYS PRECEDES A GOOD DOWNSWING, BUT A CORRECT DOWNSWING IS ALMOST IMPOSSIBLE WITHOUT A CORRECT BACKSWING.

JERK THE CLUB BACK AND YOU'VE GOT PROBLEMS. STRIVE TO SWING THE CLUB BACK VERY SMOOTHLY AND DELIBERATELY FOR THE FIRST FEW FEET. HERE AGAIN A LEAF OR TURF BLEMISH CAN BE HELPFUL. TEE UP SO THAT THE OBJECT IS A FEW FEET BEHIND AND IN LINE WITH THE BALL AND TARGET, THEN TAKE THE CLUBHEAD STRAIGHT BACK ON THIS LINE

LINE OF DIRECTION

• SETTING UP the BACKSWING •

YOU'LL FIND A SLIGHT INCLINING, OR *SETTING-IN*, OF THE RIGHT KNEE AT ADDRESS PROMOTES A FREER, EASIER BODY TURN.
WEIGHT SHIFTS EASILY AND REMAINS ON THE *INSIDE* OF THE RIGHT FOOT TO *LOCK* THE RIGHT KNEE AND PREVENT LATERAL HIP MOTION, OR SWAY.

BARRETT TAYLOR

YOU NEED SIMPLY TO TURN YOUR BODY TO BE RIGHT IN POSITION BEHIND THE BALL.

DEVELOPING A ONE-PIECE BACKSWING

THE ALL-IMPORTANT RULE FOR STARTING THE BACKSWING IS TO MOVE THE ENTIRE LEFT SIDE AWAY FROM THE BALL AT ONCE. WHEN THERE IS A STRONGER SENSATION OR PRESSURE WITH ANY ONE PART OF THE BODY, YOU ARE OFF TO A BAD START.

HOW TO ACHIEVE THIS ONE-PIECE START? A GOOD WAY IS TO CONCENTRATE ON TAKING THE CLUB BACK VERY SLOWLY DURING THE FIRST 6 INCHES OF TRAVEL AWAY FROM THE BALL.

THIS WILL HELP PREVENT ANY ONE PART OF THE BODY FROM MOVING SOONER THAN THE OTHERS AND DOMINATING THE ACTION.

MAKE SURE THERE IS NO WRIST ACTION SO AS TO KEEP THE STRAIGHT LINE FORMED BY THE LEFT ARM AND SHAFT UNBROKEN.

STARTING the BACKSWING

I TRY TO MOVE EVERYTHING AWAY FROM THE BALL AS A COMPACT *UNIT* – SMOOTHLY AND DELIBERATELY. MY GRIP IS FIRM, BUT NOT TENSE, WITH THE LEFT HAND GUIDING. THE WRISTS AND HANDS DO NOT ROTATE AND THE CLUBFACE IS HELD IN ITS ORIGINAL SQUARE POSITION.

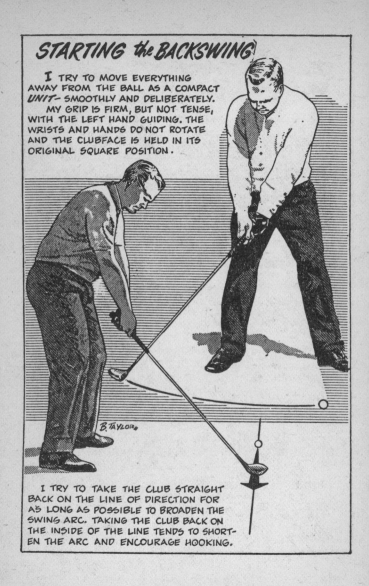

B. TAYLOR

I TRY TO TAKE THE CLUB STRAIGHT BACK ON THE LINE OF DIRECTION FOR AS LONG AS POSSIBLE TO BROADEN THE SWING ARC. TAKING THE CLUB BACK ON THE INSIDE OF THE LINE TENDS TO SHORTEN THE ARC AND ENCOURAGE HOOKING.

KEEPING TABS ON THE TAKEAWAY

IN STRIVING TO KEEP THE CLUBFACE SQUARE DURING THE TAKEAWAY, SOME PLAYERS FALL INTO A HABIT OF TURNING THE HEAD TO FOLLOW THE CLUB. AND WHEN THE HEAD MOVES, THE SWING PLANE CHANGES.

ACTUALLY, I WATCH THE CLUB-FACE MYSELF— BUT I DO SO WITHOUT MY HEAD MOVING...

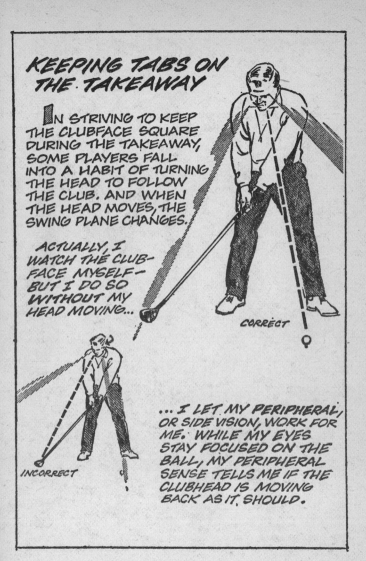

CORRECT

INCORRECT

... I LET MY PERIPHERAL, OR SIDE VISION, WORK FOR ME. WHILE MY EYES STAY FOCUSED ON THE BALL, MY PERIPHERAL SENSE TELLS ME IF THE CLUBHEAD IS MOVING BACK AS IT SHOULD.

AT THE SWING'S START IT IS HIGHLY IMPORTANT NOT TO BREAK THE WRISTS. THE LEFT ARM AND CLUBSHAFT FORMS A STRAIGHT LINE, WRISTS SERVING ONLY AS A CONNECTING LINK

MUCH DEPENDS ON THIS ONE-PIECE TAKEAWAY...IT STARTS THE SHOULDER AND BODY TURN AND KEEPS THE CLUBFACE SQUARE AND MOVING BACK ON A STRAIGHT LINE FROM THE TARGET. IT STARTS THE WHOLE SWING. SO, THE FARTHER YOU CAN TAKE THE CLUB BACK WITHOUT BREAKING THE WRISTS, THE BETTER!

WRIST BREAK on the BACKSWING

THE BACKSWING MUST BE RHYTHMICAL AND SMOOTH IN TEMPO, THEREFORE THE COCKING OF THE WRISTS MUST BE *GRADUAL*.

MOST OF THE WRIST BREAK OCCURS IN THIS AREA.

HERE THE WRISTS ARE JUST BARELY BEGINNING TO COCK.

THE WRISTS ARE NOW FULLY COCKED, AND POWER IS STORED UP TO BE RELEASED AT IMPACT.

I TRY TO TAKE THE CLUB BACK AS FAR AS POSSIBLE BEFORE THERE IS ANY EVIDENCE OF WRIST BREAK. THIS BROADENS THE SWING ARC.

NOTE THAT THE HEAD AND RIGHT LEG HAVE NOT MOVED DURING THE BACKSWING.

THERE IS NO BREAKAGE OF THE WRISTS HERE AS THE CLUB IS TAKEN BACK LOW AND STRAIGHT-AWAY.

The RIGHT ELBOW

BASICALLY, THE RIGHT ELBOW SHOULD BE HELD IN CLOSE TO THE BODY ON THE BACKSWING.

HOWEVER, THE CLOSER THE ELBOW IS TO THE BODY, THE SHORTER THE SWING ARC BECOMES. FOR THIS REASON, I ALLOW MY RIGHT ELBOW TO MOVE SLIGHTLY AWAY FROM THE BODY ON THE BACKSWING IN ORDER TO PRODUCE A WIDER ARC.

I AM NEVER CONSCIOUS OF THE ELBOW WHILE PLAYING, BUT WHEN PRACTICING CHECK TO MAKE SURE IT DOES NOT TURN OUT TOO FAR. IT MEANS TROUBLE IF THE ELBOW EVER POINTS UPWARD.

ON THE DOWNSWING, THE RIGHT ELBOW RETURNS CLOSE TO THE RIGHT SIDE.

B. TAYLOR

HOW LONG A BACKSWING?

UNDERSWING

MY POSITION

PARALLEL POSITION

OVERSWING

THERE IS NO STANDARD RULE WHICH DICTATES HOW *LONG* THE BACKSWING SHOULD BE. WHETHER A GOLFER UNDER-SWINGS OR OVERSWINGS IS, IN MY OPINION, A MATTER OF PERSONAL PREFERENCE.

COMPARE *GARY PLAYER*, WHO OVERSWINGS-TAKING THE CLUB TO ABOUT PARALLEL-WITH *DOUG SANDERS*, WHO HAS A VERY ABBREVIATED BACKSWING. BOTH ARE STRONG HITTERS.

I, MYSELF, AM ON THE SIDE OF A SHORT SWINGER, SINCE MY CLUB DOES NOT REACH PARALLEL.

CHOOSE THE LENGTH BACKSWING THAT YOU ARE MOST COMFORTABLE WITH AND WHICH SUITS YOUR PHYSICAL BUILD.

FULL SHOULDER TURN A MUST

A SMOOTH AND COMPACT SWING REQUIRES A *FULL SHOULDER TURN.* INSUFFICIENT TURN CAN DISRUPT AND CHANGE YOUR WHOLE SWING. IT WILL CAUSE YOU TO FLICK THE CLUBHEAD FROM THE TOP, HIT TOO QUICKLY AND COME OFF THE BALL.

TOO MUCH SHOULDER TURN IS BETTER THAN TOO LITTLE; THE RIGHT AMOUNT— THE CONTROLLABLE AMOUNT— CAN ADD THE NECESSARY RHYTHM TO YOUR SWING.

NOTE THAT THE TIP OF MY LEFT SHOULDER HAS REACHED A POINT ABOUT EVEN WITH MY CHIN AS THE TOP OF THE SWING IS REACHED.

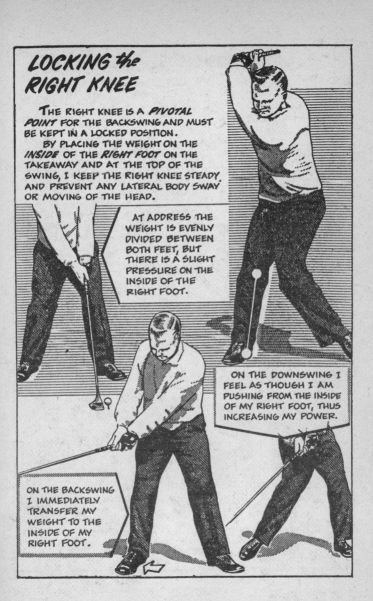

LOCKING the RIGHT KNEE

THE RIGHT KNEE IS A *PIVOTAL POINT* FOR THE BACKSWING AND MUST BE KEPT IN A LOCKED POSITION.

BY PLACING THE WEIGHT ON THE *INSIDE* OF THE *RIGHT FOOT* ON THE TAKEAWAY AND AT THE TOP OF THE SWING, I KEEP THE RIGHT KNEE STEADY AND PREVENT ANY LATERAL BODY SWAY OR MOVING OF THE HEAD.

AT ADDRESS THE WEIGHT IS EVENLY DIVIDED BETWEEN BOTH FEET, BUT THERE IS A SLIGHT PRESSURE ON THE INSIDE OF THE RIGHT FOOT.

ON THE DOWNSWING I FEEL AS THOUGH I AM PUSHING FROM THE INSIDE OF MY RIGHT FOOT, THUS INCREASING MY POWER.

ON THE BACKSWING I IMMEDIATELY TRANSFER MY WEIGHT TO THE INSIDE OF MY RIGHT FOOT.

• NO PAUSE AT TOP •

I DON'T BELIEVE IN A **PAUSE** AT THE TOP OF THE BACKSWING... I FEEL THERE MUST BE A **FLOWING**, UN-INTERRUPTED MOTION IN THE SWING. IF YOU EVER STOP AND PAUSE, YOU'RE GOING TO PRODUCE A TRICKY MOTION.

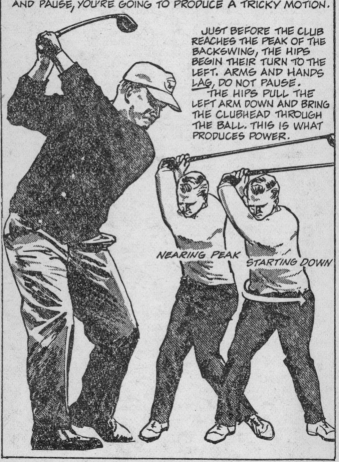

JUST BEFORE THE CLUB REACHES THE PEAK OF THE BACKSWING, THE HIPS BEGIN THEIR TURN TO THE LEFT. ARMS AND HANDS LAG, DO NOT PAUSE.

THE HIPS PULL THE LEFT ARM DOWN AND BRING THE CLUBHEAD THROUGH THE BALL. THIS IS WHAT PRODUCES POWER.

NEARING PEAK   STARTING DOWN

STARTING the DOWNSWING

TOP OF BACKSWING

BEGINNING OF DOWNSWING

MY HANDS, ARMS, AND SHOULDERS LAG BEHIND AS A *HIP TURN* AND *WEIGHT SHIFT* TO THE LEFT INITIATE THE DOWNSWING.

THE HIPS ARE ALMOST *PARALLEL* WITH THE LINE OF DIRECTION BEFORE THE CLUBHEAD STARTS TO MOVE.

THE *LEADING LEFT SIDE* CREATES A TAUTNESS THROUGH THE LEFT SHOULDER AND ARM WHICH AUTOMATICALLY KEEPS THE WRISTS COCKED FOR LEVERAGE. FROM THIS DELAYED POSITION THE HANDS CAN UNLEASH WITH A POWERFUL SLINGING, OR WHIP-LIKE ACTION THROUGH THE BALL.

• SLIDE, THEN TURN •

A COMMON QUESTION REGARDING THE START OF THE DOWNSWING IS, "SHOULD THE FIRST MOVEMENT OF THE HIPS BE LATERAL, ROTATING OR A COMBINATION?"

AS PICTURED, THE FIRST MOVE (A) IS **LATERAL** FOLLOWED BY A **ROTATION** (B) AS THE BODY SHIFT CONTINUES. YOU CANNOT, HOWEVER, CONSIDER THESE AS INDIVIDUAL ACTIONS...

... ACTIONS MUST **BLEND**, SO THAT THE SWING WILL FLOW. AFTER THE HIPS START TO ROTATE, THE LATERAL SHIFT DOES NOT CEASE, BUT CONTINUES IN UNISON UNTIL THE FINISH WHERE THE WEIGHT IS ON THE LEFT FOOT AND HIPS FACE THE TARGET.

LEAD WITH YOUR LEFT

I CANNOT OVER-EMPHASIZE THE IMPORTANCE OF *LEFT SIDE CONTROL* IN THE GOLF SWING. THE LEFT HIP INITIATES THE DOWNSWING AND THE LEFT SIDE IS STRETCHED AS FAR AS POSSIBLE AS THE CLUB-HEAD ENTERS THE HITTING AREA. THE WEIGHT HAS BEEN SHIFTED QUICKLY TO THE LEFT FOOT.

NOTE THAT THE LEFT HIP REMAINS IN APPROXIMATELY THE SAME FIXED POSITION FROM A POINT WHERE THE HANDS ARE HIP-HIGH TO THE POINT OF IMPACT. THE HANDS HAVE BEEN DELAYED UNTIL THE VERY LAST INSTANT BY A LEADING LEFT SIDE AND THEY CAN BE UNLEASHED WITH TREMENDOUS POWER FROM A WELL-BALANCED POSITION.

B. Taylor

• The RIGHT ARM AT IMPACT •

FOR MAXIMUM EXTENSION THROUGH THE HITTING AREA, BOTH ARMS MUST BE STRAIGHT FOLLOWING IMPACT. **DURING** IMPACT, HOWEVER, THE **RIGHT** ARM MUST BE SLIGHTLY BENT.

THE LEFT ARM REMAINS STRAIGHT FOR FIRMNESS AND CONTROL, BUT A STRAIGHT RIGHT AT IMPACT INDICATES THAT POWER HAS BEEN EXPELLED TOO QUICKLY.

FOR MAXIMUM CLUB ACCELERATION, MAKE SURE YOUR RIGHT ARM STRAIGHTENS JUST **AFTER** IMPACT.

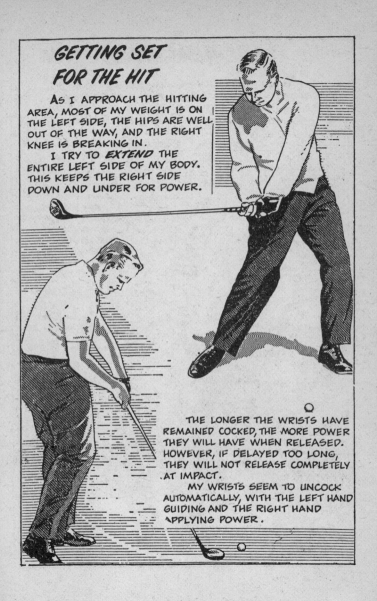

GETTING SET FOR THE HIT

As I approach the hitting area, most of my weight is on the left side, the hips are well out of the way, and the right knee is breaking in.

I try to *extend* the entire left side of my body. This keeps the right side down and under for power.

The longer the wrists have remained cocked, the more power they will have when released. However, if delayed too long, they will not release completely at impact.

My wrists seem to uncock automatically, with the left hand guiding and the right hand applying power.

The FOLLOW-THROUGH

THE FOLLOW-THROUGH IS VERY IMPORTANT, AND I FEEL IT IS OFTEN <u>MISTERMED</u> AS BEING A HIGH "PICTURE" FINISH.

ACTUALLY, THE FOLLOW-THROUGH IS DIRECTED *JUST BEFORE* THE BALL IS STRUCK, AND IS TERMINATED ABOUT *3 FEET PAST THE POINT OF IMPACT.*

BASICALLY, ONLY THE HANDS AND ARMS ARE INVOLVED. I TRY TO EXTEND *BOTH ARMS* AS FAR AS POSSIBLE BEFORE THE HANDS TURN OVER; WITH THE RIGHT ARM *POINTED* RIGHT AT THE HOLE.

AFTER THE FOLLOW-THROUGH, MOMENTUM WILL CARRY THE CLUB-HEAD NATURALLY TO A HIGH FINISH.

FOLLOW-THROUGH ENDS

B. TAYLOR

KEEP YOUR HEAD
DOWN AT THE FINISH

BECAUSE THE FINISH OF THE SWING INDICATES WHAT HAS GONE BEFORE, MAKE SURE YOUR HEAD HAS NOT LIFTED OR SWAYED FROM ITS CENTERED POSITION FOLLOWING THE HIT.

AS YOU FINISH, KEEP YOUR HEAD DOWN AND SLIGHTLY TILTED SO THAT YOU ARE WATCHING THE FLIGHT ALMOST ENTIRELY OUT OF THE CORNER OF YOUR LEFT EYE...

...THIS POSITION, ALONG WITH HIGH HANDS AND RIGHT SHOULDER BENEATH THE LEFT, SHOWS THAT YOU HAVE PERFORMED THE PRECEDING ACTIONS OF THE SWING CORRECTLY.

BARRETT TAYLOR.

FINISH NATURAL

IN DETERMINING HOW HIGH TO FINISH THE SWING WITH VARIOUS CLUBS, CONSIDER THE NATURAL FINISH AS BEST.

THE WEDGE FINISH WILL NORMALLY BE LOWER THAN THAT OF THE DRIVER, DUE TO A SHORTER BACKSWING AND EXTRA HAND ACTION NECESSARY AT IMPACT...

WEDGE

DRIVER

LET THE LENGTH OF THE BACKSWING DICTATE THE GENERAL HEIGHT TO THE FINISH. A HIGH SHORT IRON FINISH IS FINE IF NOT FORCED, BUT HANDS SHOULDER HIGH IS GENERALLY THE ACCEPTED NATURAL ENDING POSITION WITH THE WEDGE, 8 AND 9 IRONS. BE SURE TO STOP NO LOWER ON FULL SHOTS.

CHAPTER 3

Hitting For Distance

The big thing to remember when you're reaching for extra yards is not to over-reach your own capabilities. Many golfers faced with a long, difficult shot often tense up and make a conscious effort to hit the ball harder. Thus, in their hurry to get back to the ball, they rush their backswing, fail to make a full pivot, and use up most of their power before the actual hit. The result is a weak, ineffectual shot not worthy of the best in you.

Distance through power is achieved by building up clubhead speed, not by consciously trying to muscle the ball. Greater clubhead speed is created by widening the arc of your swing. Nothing else should change. But by deliberately trying to hit the ball harder, you will throw off your timing and coordination, the very ingredients that are so vital in producing a true hit.

Of course, you must try to hit the ball harder when you're looking for added distance, but it must be done within the framework of your regular swing. If you have maintained a rhythmic, controlled swing throughout, it is only inevitable that your hands will be moving faster at impact than they were when you began your downswing. Now the result will be a shot that will literally fly off your clubhead.

In digesting the panels I have prepared for this section, there should be one pervading thought in your mind: be sure to play within yourself at all times.

• ADDING YARDAGE •

THE MAJORITY OF GOLFERS CAN GAIN EXTRA DISTANCE MERELY BY TAKING THE HANDS *HIGHER* ON THE BACKSWING.

THE HIGHER THE HANDS AT THE TOP, THE LONGER THE ARC; HENCE, THE GREATER THE FORCE AND MOMENTUM OF THE DOWNSWING.

THE HANDS SHOULD REACH HIGHER THAN SHOULDER LEVEL, BUT FEW AVERAGE GOLFERS ATTAIN EVEN A SHOULDER-HIGH POSITION.

NOTE THAT MY HANDS ARE SLIGHTLY ABOVE THE TOP OF MY HEAD.

CHECK THE TOP OF YOUR OWN SWING. IF YOUR HANDS ARE TOO LOW, *FORCE* THEM HIGHER. IT WILL PAY A DIVIDEND OF DISTANCE.

BARRETT TAYLOR.

56

TEE HIGH for DISTANCE

TEEING THE BALL ALMOST AS HIGH AS POSSIBLE FOR THE DRIVER ENABLES ME TO HIT SLIGHTLY ON THE *UPSWING* AND CATCH THE BALL FLUSH NEAR THE *TOP* OF THE CLUBFACE.

THE RESULT IS A *HIGH CARRYING BALL* WHICH, IN MY OPINION, WILL COVER GREATER DISTANCE THAN ONE TEED SHORT AND HIT LOW.

BY CONTRAST, IRON SHOTS SHOULD BE TEED LOW, SINCE THE BALL MUST BE STRUCK NEAR THE *BOTTOM* OF THE FACE WITH A MORE *DESCENDING* BLOW.

DRIVER...

IRONS...

BARRETT TAYLOR.

• TWO POINTS for POWER •

THERE ARE TWO PHASES TO BUILDING POWER ON THE BACKSWING. THE FIRST IS THE COMPLETE COILING OF THE BODY, THE SECOND INVOLVES **STRETCHING** . . .

. . . FOR AS YOU COIL YOU MUST AT THE SAME TIME STRETCH THE LEFT SIDE. YOU SHOULD FEEL AS THOUGH YOU ARE STRETCHING YOUR LEFT ARM AS FAR AS POSSIBLE IN TAKING THE CLUB BACK AND AS HIGH AS POSSIBLE IN REACHING THE TOP OF THE SWING.

THE FARTHER YOU COIL AND STRETCH, THE LARGER YOUR SWING ARC BECOMES, AND THE GREATER THE CLUBHEAD SPEED BECOMES AT IMPACT.

A SMALL MOVE THAT MAKES A BIG DIFFERENCE

●

WANT EXTRA DISTANCE WITHOUT EXTRA EFFORT? IF SO, SIMPLY TURN YOUR SHOULDERS A LITTLE FARTHER ON THE BACKSWING.

THIS EXTRA COILING CREATES A GREATER SWING ARC AND THEREBY PRODUCES GREATER LEVERAGE. AND THE MORE LEVERAGE GAINED, THE MORE CLUBSPEED POSSIBLE DURING THE RELEASE.

THE RESULTS OF THAT LITTLE EXTRA TURN WILL REVEAL THAT POWER DEPENDS MAINLY ON A FULL, FREE SWING AND A DELAYED HITTING ACTION, NOT UPON A FORCED, SPEED-UP TEMPO.

POWER PLUS,

GETTING the MOST out of YOUR DRIVER

How many times have you heard the words, "Hit it nice and *EASY*, now!", directed to a player with a driver in his hands? In heeding such advice, the average golfer is often influenced toward a loose, lazy swing which robs him of both control and distance.

A better maxim would be "Hit it nice and *SMOOTHLY*, now!" for if there is proper *RHYTHM* and *TIMING* to the swing, the golfer can hit as hard as he wants to.

I hit *HARD* on all of my drives, and if I want more distance, I hit *HARDER*.

Still, I swing well "within" myself; never so recklessly all out that I lose balance or control of the club.

I never swing hard with the irons, where accuracy is more vital than distance. The swing should be easy, yet firm.

SWING HARD.. .. SWING EASY

60

SHOULDERS OUT-TURN HIPS

A GOOD RULE TO REMEMBER IN ACHIEVING PROPER BODY TURN DURING THE BACKSWING IS THAT THE **SHOULDERS** MUST ALWAYS TURN FARTHER THAN THE HIPS, REGARDLESS OF CLUB OR TYPE OF SHOT

MAKE THE BODY TURN UNTIL THE HIPS HAVE ROTATED AS FAR AS THEY CAN, THEN CONTINUE TO TURN THE SHOULDERS TO MAXIMUM. THIS WILL GIVE YOU THE PROPER HIP AND SHOULDER RELATION AS REQUIRED IN DRIVING. THIS CREATES THE LEVERAGE AND LONG SWING ARC NECESSARY FOR MAXIMUM POWER AND CONTROL ON THE DOWNSWING.

POSITIONING the LEFT FOOT for EXTRA YARDS

ONE SLIGHT ADJUSTMENT THAT HAS ENABLED ME TO BETTER UTILIZE MY BODY AND GAIN EXTRA DISTANCE HAS BEEN THE POSITIONING OF MY **LEFT FOOT.** INSTEAD OF POINTING THE FOOT AT THE CONVENTIONAL **30°** ANGLE TOWARD A LINE PARALLEL WITH THE TARGET, I TURN IT A LITTLE MORE TO THE LEFT AT ABOUT A **45°** ANGLE.

45°

30°

DIRECTION

B. TAYLOR

(THE RIGHT FOOT IS JUST A SHADE TO THE RIGHT OF BEING SQUARE TO THE LINE OF DIRECTION.)

THIS LEFT FOOT LOCATION ALLOWS MY HIPS TO TURN FASTER WITHOUT RESTRICTION AND GET OUT OF THE WAY QUICKLY AS I REACH THE HITTING AREA. THE ACCELERATION OF THE CLUBHEAD IS UNINTERRUPTED AND I CAN GET MY WHOLE BODY BEHIND THE SHOT.

USE YOUR LEGS for POWER

MAXIMUM SWING POWER IS POSSIBLE ONLY THROUGH PROPER LEG ACTION; FOR HIPS CAN PULL THE ARMS JUST SO FAR, THEN THE LEGS MUST TAKE OVER.

AT THE TOP   STARTING DOWN

BARRETT TAYLOR

EVEN AS THE DOWNSWING BEGINS, LEGS ASSIST THE HIP—TURN AND WEIGHT-SHIFT TO THE LEFT.

HALFWAY DOWN THE LEGS COME INTO FULL PLAY, GENERATING A TREMENDOUS THRUST THAT PUSHES THE ARMS AND HIPS THROUGH TO THE FINISH.

USING YOUR LEGS

LEGS SUPPLY MUCH OF THE POWER IN GOLF SERVING AS A THRUSTING AGENT TO SEND BODY, ARMS AND SHOULDERS THROUGH THE BALL. TENSE AND STIFF, THE LEGS FAIL IN THIS FUNCTION. LOOSE AND OVERLY-RELAXED, THEY LIKEWISE LACK IMPETUS.

THUS, A HAPPY MEDIUM IS REQUIRED. THE LEGS MUST BE FLEXED OR BENT, SLIGHTLY AT ADDRESS TO REMOVE TENSION, YET THEY MUST RETAIN A FEELING OF FIRMNESS.

BARRETT TAYLOR

STEADY, YET PASSIVE, THE LEGS MUST BE POISED AND READY TO MOVE FREELY, AS THOUGH YOU WERE GETTING SET TO RUN THE 100 YD. DASH.

• FAIRWAY WOODS •

THE HARDEST CLUBS FOR THE AVERAGE GOLFER TO MASTER ARE THE LONG IRONS— AND WITH THE INCREASING POPULARITY OF THE EASIER-TO-HIT 5 WOOD, AND FAIRWAY WOODS IN GENERAL, THE QUESTION OFTEN ARISES: "SHOULD THE WOOD AND IRON SWINGS DIFFER?"

THE ANSWER IS SIMPLE. PLAY THE FAIRWAY WOOD EXACTLY LIKE AN IRON. HIT DOWN AND THROUGH. LET THE CLUBHEAD STRIKE THE BALL FIRST, THEN THE TURF IN THE DIVOT- TAKING MANNER.

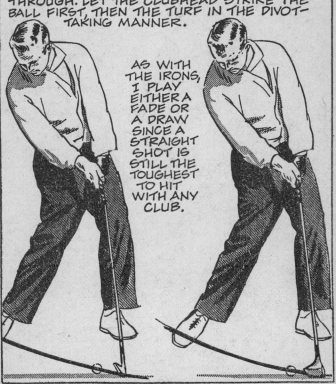

AS WITH THE IRONS, I PLAY EITHER A FADE OR A DRAW SINCE A STRAIGHT SHOT IS STILL THE TOUGHEST TO HIT WITH ANY CLUB.

• POWER IS THROUGHOUT •

ONE OF THE GREATEST MISCONCEPTIONS CONCERNING POWER IS THE IDEA THAT IT CAN BE TURNED ON OR OFF.

THERE IS NO SPECIAL AREA ALONG THE SWING'S ROUTE WHERE POWER IS CONSCIOUSLY RELEASED. *POWER IS THROUGHOUT*...

... POWER COMES FROM A SMOOTH BLENDING OF ALL COMPONENTS FROM START TO FINISH SO THAT THE CLUBHEAD GRADUALLY REACHES FULL VELOCITY AT IMPACT.

MAKE A CONSCIOUS EFFORT TO THROW THE CLUBHEAD AT THE BALL AND YOU WILL DEVELOP TROUBLE. STRIVE FOR A RHYTHMICAL, FLOWING STROKE AND YOU WILL DEVELOP POWER.

CHAPTER 4

Irons Play

The secret to good irons play is consistency. Whether you are hitting a two-iron or a nine-iron, the idea is to hit every shot in the same manner, *with the same tempo*. The only significant differences, of course, are in the length of the backswing and the amount of body action you put into the shot.

With the long-irons, where you're striving for distance, you should take a full backswing and follow through. With the shorter irons, where your goal is accuracy more than length, you don't need as much backswing or body pivot. Otherwise, the swing always remains the same.

Still, high-handicap golfers have the most difficulty with their long-irons. This problem is understandable, because the two-, three- and four-irons have longer shafts and shallower faces than the higher-numbered irons do, and it makes them feel they have to work harder to achieve a proper shot. They become scared to use their normal swing and turn to artificial methods, such as the ones I've outlined in this section.

Since tempo plays such an important part in your overall irons game, let me give you a few pointers on how to develop and maintain it. Tempo varies with the individual; so, to discover your own tempo, try swinging a club with your left arm only. This will help you achieve a certain rhythm on your take-away and downswing. After swinging in this tempo several times, place your right hand on the club and let it follow the action without disturbing the motion of the left arm. This should be your tempo, and it should be identical on both your backswing and your downswing. Don't let the length—or difficulty—of the iron alter it.

HITTING the LONG IRONS

THE MAJORITY OF PLAYERS WHO MIS-HIT THE LONG IRONS MAKE THE MISTAKE OF **POUNDING DOWN** ON THE SHOT.

OFTEN, IN THE DIVOT-TAKING PROCESS, THEY EITHER STOP THE CLUB IN THE GROUND OR HIT "FAT" BEHIND THE BALL.

YOU MUST **SWEEP** THE BALL WITH THESE CLUBS...TRY TO KEEP THE CLUBHEAD **LOW** AT IMPACT SO IT STRIKES THE BACK OF THE BALL SOLIDLY THEN CONTINUES THROUGH WITHOUT CATCHING GROUND. THE RESULT WILL BE BETTER LOFT AND GREATER CONSISTENCY.

SWING A LONG IRON LIKE A SHORT IRON

9 IRON   2 IRON

MOST PLAYERS MISTAKENLY TRY TO *POWER* THE LONG IRONS. THEY'VE HEARD HOW ALLEGEDLY "TOUGH" THESE CLUBS ARE — HENCE, THEY FEEL THE SWING MUST BE EXTRA HARD.

IN REALITY, THE SWING FOR A 2 IRON SHOULD BE NO HARDER THAN THE SWING FOR THE 9 IRON!

I APPLY THE SAME AMOUNT OF POWER THROUGH THE BALL WITH **ALL** IRONS. THE SWING MERELY BECOMES A LITTLE LONGER AS THE CLUB LENGTHS INCREASE.

HIT A FEW 9 IRON SHOTS, THEN PICK UP YOUR 2 IRON AND SWING NO HARDER AT THE BALL, AND SEE THE RESULTS.

• FOR CLEAN CONTACT, TEE UP •

IN PLAYING IRONS TO PAR 3 HOLES, ALWAYS TEE THE BALL. THE GOLFER WHO SHUNS A TEE AND HITS DIRECTLY FROM TURF RUNS THE RISK OF GRASS COMING BETWEEN THE CLUBFACE AND THE BALL... AND WHEN THIS OCCURS HE MAY SEE HIS BALL TAKE SOME ODD TURNS—USUALLY FOR THE WORSE.

PREVENT THIS

BY THIS

BARRETT TAYLOR

MY BALL IS TEED LOW, BUT HIGH ENOUGH TO AVOID GRASS PROBLEM.

• TEE HIGH TO LOFT AN IRON •

WHEN IT IS DESIRABLE TO HIT A LONG IRON FROM THE TEE WITH AS MUCH HEIGHT AND CARRY AS POSSIBLE, *TEE THE BALL HIGH* .

TRUE, YOU GENERALLY TEE LOW FOR IRONS TO FACILITATE HITTING DOWN AND TAKING TURF FOR BACKSPIN, BUT THE IDEA HERE IS NOT TO TAKE A DIVOT BUT TO STRIKE THE BALL SOLIDLY AT THE BOTTOM OF THE SWING WITH A *SWEEPING*, RATHER THAN A DESCENDING, MOTION.

BARRETT TAYLOR

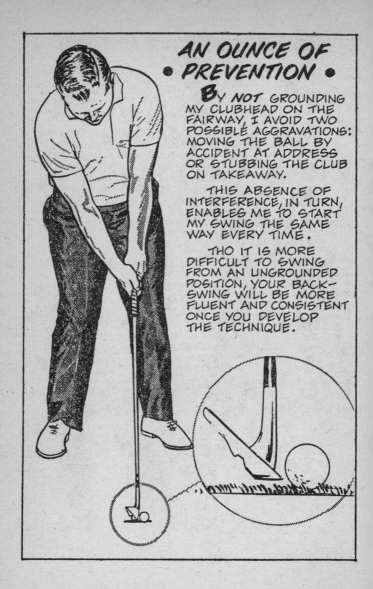

AN OUNCE OF • PREVENTION •

BY *NOT* GROUNDING MY CLUBHEAD ON THE FAIRWAY, I AVOID TWO POSSIBLE AGGRAVATIONS: MOVING THE BALL BY ACCIDENT AT ADDRESS OR STUBBING THE CLUB ON TAKEAWAY.

THIS ABSENCE OF INTERFERENCE, IN TURN, ENABLES ME TO START MY SWING THE SAME WAY EVERY TIME.

THO IT IS MORE DIFFICULT TO SWING FROM AN UNGROUNDED POSITION, YOUR BACK-SWING WILL BE MORE FLUENT AND CONSISTENT ONCE YOU DEVELOP THE TECHNIQUE.

MIDDLE IRONS KEY FOR
• PRACTICE •

THE PRACTICE METHOD OF HITTING MID-IRONS TO HELP CURE SHORT IRON TROUBLES CAN ALSO APPLY TO A LAGGING LONG IRON GAME.

THE BASIC CAUSE OF DIFFICULTY WITH LONG IRONS STEMS FROM THE ASSUMPTION THAT THESE CLUBS DEMAND A SPEED-UP TEMPO AND A HARDER HIT. ACTUALLY, THE SWING, THOUGH SLIGHTLY LONGER, SHOULD BE EXACTLY OF THE SAME TEMPO AS THE SHORTER CLUB SWING

SINCE TEMPO COMES EASIEST WITH THE MID-IRONS, FIRST PRACTICE SHOTS USING A 4, 5 OR 6 IRON, THEN WHEN THE SWING HAS SMOOTHED OUT, GO BACK TO THE LONG IRON AND SWING THE SAME. KEEP SWITCHING FROM MIDDLE TO LONG IRON UNTIL TEMPO IS ESTABLISHED.

5 IRON

2 IRON

(FOR THESE REASONS I PRACTICE THE MID-IRONS MOST.)

CHAPTER 5

The Short Game

While strong drives and consistent approach shots enable you to attack a golf course, you don't really settle your score with it unless you can pitch and chip effectively when you come within hailing distance of the green. This is where you save yourself strokes on your scorecard—on the strength and precision of your short game.

Since the principle behind pitching and chipping is to get the ball close enough to the hole to allow for the fewest number of putts, accuracy here is of the utmost importance. Selecting the correct club for a given shot is just as critical as knowing how to play the shot. As a general rule, I approach chipping situations this way: the longer the chip must travel, the lower I want the ball to run. Thus, I use a longer-shafted club which will produce a low trajectory. (But I never chip with anything lower than a five-iron, because I wouldn't get the delicate control I need with the two-, three- or four-irons.) The closer I am to the hole, the more I'm inclined to go with a shorter-shafted club with a deep face.

Of all the clubs in the bag, the wedge is the easiest to hit, but the hardest to play. This is so because it places a greater premium on accuracy than any of the other clubs do. I play a full wedge from about 105 yards in, but I advise average players to use it only when they get as close as 80 yards from the pin. Your swing with the wedge should be a little more upright than it is with the other clubs. This allows the club to descend at a sharper angle, producing a knifing action and creating greater loft and backspin necessary to stop the ball quickly when it lands on the green—hopefully, right next to the pin.

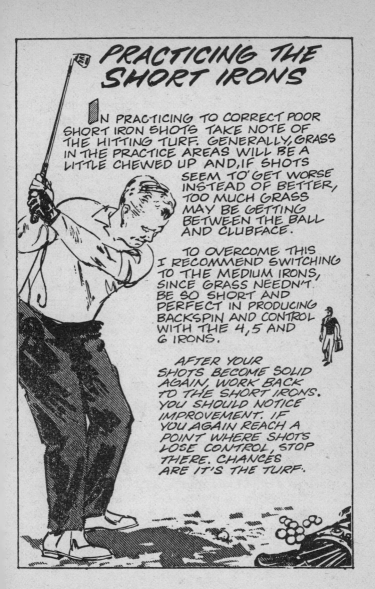

PRACTICING THE SHORT IRONS

IN PRACTICING TO CORRECT POOR SHORT IRON SHOTS TAKE NOTE OF THE HITTING TURF. GENERALLY, GRASS IN THE PRACTICE AREAS WILL BE A LITTLE CHEWED UP AND, IF SHOTS SEEM TO GET WORSE INSTEAD OF BETTER, TOO MUCH GRASS MAY BE GETTING BETWEEN THE BALL AND CLUBFACE.

TO OVERCOME THIS I RECOMMEND SWITCHING TO THE MEDIUM IRONS, SINCE GRASS NEEDN'T BE SO SHORT AND PERFECT IN PRODUCING BACKSPIN AND CONTROL WITH THE 4, 5 AND 6 IRONS.

AFTER YOUR SHOTS BECOME SOLID AGAIN, WORK BACK TO THE SHORT IRONS. YOU SHOULD NOTICE IMPROVEMENT. IF YOU AGAIN REACH A POINT WHERE SHOTS LOSE CONTROL, STOP THERE. CHANCES ARE IT'S THE TURF.

The CHIP SHOT

BASICALLY, I TRY TO HIT AN *ALL WRIST* CHIP; ESPECIALLY IN CHIPPING FROM THE FRINGE; WITHOUT ANY ARM MOTION.

THE STANCE IS SLIGHTLY OPEN WITH THE FEET CLOSE TOGETHER.

MOST OF THE WEIGHT IS ON THE LEFT FOOT THROUGHOUT.

THE MOST IMPORTANT THING IN CHIPPING IS TO USE AN *EASY, FIRM,* AND *SLOW* SWING. THIS IS THE HARDEST THING I'VE HAD TO LEARN, AND AM STILL LEARNING.

I FEEL THAT ONCE I CAN CONSISTENTLY EMPLOY A SLOW, EASY, FIRM MOTION, I WILL BE A MUCH IMPROVED CHIPPER.

BE SURE THE SWING IS SMOOTH AND RHYTHMICAL AND THAT YOU HIT THROUGH THE BALL WITHOUT STOPPING.

B.TAYLOR,

DEVELOPING CHIPPING TECHNIQUE

THE MAIN PURPOSE IN PRACTICING CHIPS SHOULD BE TO DEVELOP **TECHNIQUE.** IF YOU CONCENTRATE MERELY ON MOVING QUICKLY FROM ONE SHOT TO ANOTHER OF VARYING DISTANCE FOR 'TOUCH' PURPOSES, YOU WILL GAIN LITTLE OVERALL PLAYING TECHNIQUE.

MY SYSTEM IS TO FIRST SELECT A GOOD LIE AND HIT ONE KIND OF SHOT UNTIL I CAN PRODUCE THE SAME ACTION EVERY TIME. THEN I CAN WORRY ABOUT HOW HARD OR EASY TO HIT TO VARY LENGTH. DOING THIS FOR EVERY TYPE SHOT WILL EVENTUALLY LEAD TO SOUND PLAY UNDER PRESSURE.

The HIGH, SHORT CHIP

@NE PARTICULARLY DELICATE SHOT THAT OFTEN ARISES IS THE SHORT WEDGE CHIP THAT MUST RISE TO CLEAR A TRAP OR HEAVY FRINGE AND STOP QUICKLY.

BECAUSE OF THE EASY SWING, THE TENDENCY IS TO QUIT ON THE SHOT OR TO SKULL IT...

.. MY METHOD OF HANDLING THE SITUATION IS TO **OPEN** THE CLUBFACE A BIT AT ADDRESS...

... THIS LETS ME TAKE A SLIGHTLY LONGER SWING THAN IS NORMALLY PERMITTED BUT STILL GET THE SAME DISTANCE. THE PRINCIPLE BEING, *THE HARDER YOU CAN SWING AT THE BALL, THE EASIER IT IS TO HIT.*

STILL, YOU NEED NERVE. YOU CAN'T QUIT ON THIS SHOT. KEEP YOUR EYE RIGHT ON TOP OF THAT BALL AND STRIKE IT SOLIDLY.

KEEP BODY OUT OF CHIP

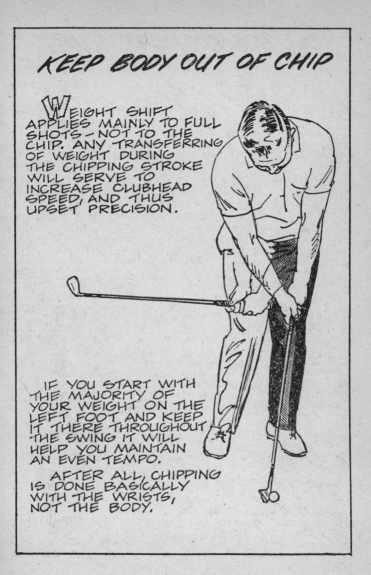

WEIGHT SHIFT APPLIES MAINLY TO FULL SHOTS – NOT TO THE CHIP. ANY TRANSFERRING OF WEIGHT DURING THE CHIPPING STROKE WILL SERVE TO INCREASE CLUBHEAD SPEED, AND THUS UPSET PRECISION.

IF YOU START WITH THE MAJORITY OF YOUR WEIGHT ON THE LEFT FOOT AND KEEP IT THERE THROUGHOUT THE SWING IT WILL HELP YOU MAINTAIN AN EVEN TEMPO.

AFTER ALL, CHIPPING IS DONE BASICALLY WITH THE WRISTS, NOT THE BODY.

GRIP FIRMLY for SOLID CHIPPING

SOME PLAYERS FEEL THEY SHOULD HOLD THE CLUB MORE TIGHTLY FOR CHIPPING. OTHERS THINK A LOOSE GRIP IS BEST... **BOTH** GROUPS ARE WRONG.

THE GRIP MUST BE EXACTLY THE SAME AS FOR FULL SHOTS — **FIRM**, BUT NOT VISE-LIKE, TO ASSURE A SMOOTH, EVEN STROKE AND CRISP CONTACT.

BARRETT TAYLOR

THE MOST IMPORTANT THING TO REMEMBER IS THAT A CHIP MUST BE STRUCK **SOLIDLY**. THIS CANNOT BE ACCOMPLISHED WITH A TIGHT GRIP AND A CHOPPY SWING OR A LOOSE GRIP AND A FLOPPY MOTION.

CHOKE DOWN for CHIPS

ONE OF THE IMPORTANT THINGS TO REMEMBER IN CHIPPING AND PITCHING IS THAT A GRIPPING DOWN ON THE CLUB MAKES IT EASIER TO HIT THE BALL, THUS INCREASES CONTROL.

A GREAT MANY PLAYERS MISTAKENLY GRIP HIGH ON THE CLUB IN THE MANNER OF HITTING FULL SHOTS.

I FEEL THAT SHOTS AS DELICATE AS THESE DEMAND MAXIMUM CONTROL OF THE CLUBHEAD, AND THIS IS BEST ACHIEVED BY KEEPING THE HANDS AND CLUBHEAD AS CLOSELY RELATED AS POSSIBLE.

HANDS TAKE THE LEAD in CHIPPING

IN CHIPPING AND PITCHING, AS IN ANY SHOT, YOUR STARTING POSITION WILL LARGELY DETERMINE YOUR IMPACT POSITION.

THUS, FOR THESE SHORT SHOTS THE HANDS MUST BE WELL AHEAD OF THE CLUBHEAD AT ADDRESS.

THIS PLACES THE HANDS IN A POSITION TO LEAD THE ENTIRE STROKE — TO STAY AHEAD OF THE CLUBHEAD DURING THE HIT AND ASSURE THAT THE BALL WILL BE STRUCK FIRST, THEN THE TURF!

DON'T TRY TO SCOOP THE BALL UP BY ALLOWING THE CLUBHEAD TO PASS THE HANDS. HIT *DOWN* SHARPLY WITH THE HANDS FORWARD AND THE CLUB'S BUILT-IN LOFT WILL RAISE THE BALL.

ADDRESS

IMPACT

BALL CLOSE for CHIPS

ONE OF THE MOST IMPORTANT POINTS IN GOOD CHIPPING IS TO POSITION THE FEET RELATIVELY CLOSE TO THE BALL. WHEN THE BODY IS TOO FAR FROM THE BALL THE SWING ARC BECOMES FLAT AND THE CLUBHEAD TRAVELS IN AN OPEN-TO-SHUT MANNER, PRODUCING A WISHY-WASHY TYPE OF ACTION THROUGH IMPACT.

THE CLOSER THE BALL IS TO THE FEET THE MORE UPRIGHT THE SWING WILL BECOME, AND THE SQUARER THE CLUB-FACE WILL REMAIN THROUGHOUT THE ARC.

THE CLUB CAN BE PICKED UP ABRUPTLY AND BROUGHT DOWN SHARPLY INTO THE BALL FOR MORE CONSISTENT BACKSPIN AND CONTROL.

AS SHOWN HERE THE CLUBHEAD REMAINS ON THE LINE OF DIRECTION LONGER AND MORE PRECISELY THROUGHOUT THE SWING.

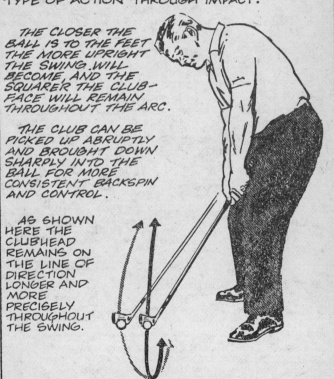

GAUGING the CHIP

Generally, in chipping or pitching, I will try to choose a club that will allow the ball to land on a spot **4** or **5** feet onto the green and roll the rest of the way.

If I am **20** yds. from the landing spot and the ball must roll **20** yds. after it lands, I will use about a **9** iron, since the ball will run about as far as it is hit with this club. If I am only **5** yds. away, I will use a **5** or **6** iron, because the ball will run a lot farther than it is hit.

With a wedge, however, I will often pitch the ball up closer to the hole, since the higher degree of backspin produced will stop it sooner.

9 IRON   6 IRON

EXPERIMENT WITH EACH CLUB AND NOTE HOW FAR THE BALL WILL RUN IN RELATION TO THE DISTANCE IT IS HIT. TRY TO BE VERSATILE IN CHIPPING. DON'T RELY ON JUST ONE OR TWO CLUBS FOR ALL DISTANCES.

PITCHING WITH THE 8 IRON

ANOTHER USE FOR THE 8 IRON ARISES WHEN GREENS ARE SLICK AND STRONG CROSSWINDS THREATEN THE LOFTED PITCH

HERE THE WEDGE PROVIDES A 'SOMETIMES' SHOT. THE BALL MAY OR MAY NOT GET BACK TO THE HOLE; AND IN TRYING TO APPLY BACKSPIN YOU MAY OCCASIONALLY FLUFF THE SHOT SLIGHTLY AND GET OVERSPIN.

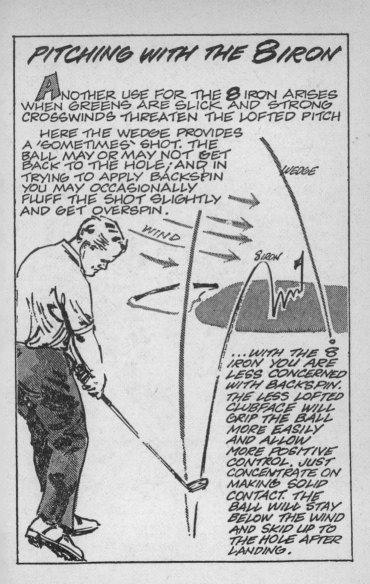

WIND

WEDGE

8 IRON

...WITH THE 8 IRON YOU ARE LESS CONCERNED WITH BACKSPIN. THE LESS LOFTED CLUBFACE WILL GRIP THE BALL MORE EASILY AND ALLOW MORE POSITIVE CONTROL. JUST CONCENTRATE ON MAKING SOLID CONTACT. THE BALL WILL STAY BELOW THE WIND AND SKID UP TO THE HOLE AFTER LANDING.

TWO WAYS TO HANDLE ROUGH

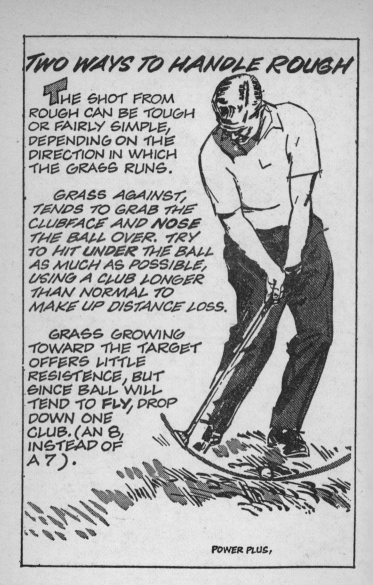

THE SHOT FROM ROUGH CAN BE TOUGH OR FAIRLY SIMPLE, DEPENDING ON THE DIRECTION IN WHICH THE GRASS RUNS.

GRASS AGAINST, TENDS TO GRAB THE CLUBFACE AND **NOSE** THE BALL OVER. TRY TO **HIT UNDER** THE BALL AS MUCH AS POSSIBLE, USING A CLUB LONGER THAN NORMAL TO MAKE UP DISTANCE LOSS.

GRASS GROWING TOWARD THE TARGET OFFERS LITTLE RESISTENCE, BUT SINCE BALL WILL TEND TO **FLY,** DROP DOWN ONE CLUB. (AN 8, INSTEAD OF A 7).

POWER PLUS,

WHEN A 9 IRON IS BETTER THAN A WEDGE

WHEN I AM WEDGE DISTANCE AWAY AND THE WIND'S AGAINST, I FIND THAT A 9 IRON IS QUITE OFTEN THE BETTER CLUB TO PLAY.

LESS LOFT MEANS GREATER CONTROL IN MOST ANY CASE. WITH A 2 IRON, FOR EXAMPLE, IT IS MUCH EASIER TO START THE BALL STRAIGHT FOR THE FIRST 50 YDS. THAN IT IS WITH A WEDGE.

WEDGE
9 IRON

WHERE I WOULD NORMALLY USE A 3/4 SWING WITH THE WEDGE, I'LL PLAY A 1/2 SWING 9 IRON—AND WITH THE HEAD-WIND, STOPPING THE BALL IS NO PROBLEM

WHEN THE WIND BLOWS, KEEP IT LOW.

PLAYING The WEDGE

TO MAINTAIN GOOD BALANCE AND CONTROL WITH THE WEDGE, THE FEET SHOULD REMAIN *FLAT* THROUGHOUT THE SWING—NO LIFTING OF THE LEFT HEEL OR ROLLING THE LEFT FOOT, EXCEPT THAT THE RIGHT HEEL WILL LIFT SLIGHTLY ON THE FOLLOW-THROUGH.

WITH THE WEDGE THE WEIGHT IS ON THE *LEFT FOOT* AT ADDRESS AND SHOULD BASICALLY BE LEFT THERE THROUGHOUT THE SWING. A SLIGHT WEIGHT SHIFT TO THE RIGHT NATURALLY OCCURS ON THE BACKSWING, BUT A CONSCIOUS EFFORT SHOULD BE MADE TO KEEP IT ON THE LEFT. THIS ENABLES YOU TO COME INTO THE BALL ABRUPTLY.

WEIGHT TO LEFT

FEET FLAT

RIGHT FOOT LIFTS SLIGHTLY

B. TAYLOR

The SHORT WEDGE SHOT

FEW SHOTS IN GOLF COME TOUGHER THAN THE SHORT, OR HALF, WEDGE FROM ABOUT 50 YARDS. ALONG WITH PLENTY OF PRACTICE IT REQUIRES *CONSISTENCY OF STROKE.*

YOU CAN HIT THEM HARD OR EASY, BUT YOU MUST HIT THEM THE SAME WAY EVERY TIME. YOU'LL NEVER GET THE PROPER "FEEL" WITH A SWING THAT VARIES.

AVERAGE GOLFERS WILL FIND THE HARD-HITTING STYLE BEST. THIS LESSENS THE TENDENCY TO LET-UP AND "SOFT" THE SHOT.

ALSO, BE SURE THE BACKSWING IS LONG ENOUGH TO PREVENT JABBING AT THE BALL, AND SHORT ENOUGH TO AVOID OVERSHOOTING THE TARGET.

The SAFETY WEDGE SHOT

A SHORT RECOVERY SHOT THAT MUST CLEAR A MOUND OR TRAP AND STOP QUICKLY REQUIRES A SLOW, EASY SWING WITH FIRM HAND CONTROL...

... OPEN THE FACE OF YOUR WEDGE, GRIP FIRMLY WITH YOUR LEFT HAND AND DIRECT THE HIT WITH YOUR RIGHT. THIS CAUSES THE BALL TO RISE QUICKLY AND LAND SOFTLY.

OPEN CLUBFACE

HIT WITH RIGHT HAND

UNLESS WINNING DEPENDS ON GETTING CLOSE TO THE PIN, THIS SHOT, PLAYED WELL AWAY FROM THE DANGER, WILL SAVE STROKES IN THE LONG RUN. WITH A GOOD PUTT YOU CAN STILL SALVAGE A PAR

SIMPLIFYING SHOTS AROUND THE GREEN

CHANGING CHIPPING CLUBS FROM SHOT TO SHOT PRESENTS TWO VARIABLES. ONE IS *LOFT*, THE OTHER IS *HOW HARD TO HIT*.

YOU CAN SIMPLIFY MATTERS BY STICKING TO ONLY *TWO* CLUBS FOR MOST CHIPS. THAT IS, A CLUB (SUCH AS A WEDGE) FOR *LOFT* SHOTS, AND CLUB (LIKE A 6-IRON) FOR *RUNNING* SHOTS.

...A CLUB FOR LOFTING

...A CLUB FOR RUNNING

SINCE ONE CLUB IS EASIER TO MASTER THAN SEVERAL, PREDICTING RESULTS WILL COME EASIER AND MAKE FOR CONSISTENCY. OF COURSE, CONDITIONS WILL NOT ALWAYS ALLOW USING YOUR 'PET' CLUB, BUT IF GIVEN A CHOICE, TAKE IT.

ONE CLUB FOR ALL CHIPS? WHY NOT?

BOBBY LOCKE, ONE OF THE GREATEST CHIPPERS THE GAME HAS KNOWN, USES ONE CLUB FOR ALL TYPES OF CHIP SHOTS. HE IS MASTER OF THE *PITCHING WEDGE* FROM ANYWHERE TO 6 INCHES OFF THE PUTTING SURFACE.

FRANKLY, THAT IS HOW I WOULD LIKE TO CHIP, THOUGH PRESENTLY I VARY MY CLUBS FOR DIFFERENT CONDITIONS.

BUT I POSITIVELY RECOMMEND THIS ONE CLUB IDEA FOR WEEK-END GOLFERS. ONE CLUB — WHETHER THE WEDGE, 9 OR 8 IRON — IS EASIER TO MASTER THAN SEVERAL, THUS WILL OFFER BEST OVERALL RESULTS.

CHAPTER 6

Bunker Shots

One of the simplest shots for a pro to make, but one of the hardest for the average player to pull off is recovering from sand. Of course, the pro knows he can get out of a trap—all he's concentrating on is getting as close to the hole as possible. The poor week-ender is just praying he can get out, period.

There are two logical reasons why the average player finds bunker play so hazardous. The first is that this is the one shot he never gets to practice away from the golf course. The only time he gets to play from sand is when he finds his ball in a trap during a round, and then it's too late to think of practice. The second reason is that he finds it difficult to accept the fact that this is the one shot where he doesn't actually have to hit the ball, and he just can't make himself go through with it.

Well, believe it, because it's true. If you would just bear in mind that the action of taking sand an inch or two behind the ball will create sufficient pressure to explode the ball out of there, half your mental block will be cured. The other half will be relieved if you simply remember to follow through, instead of stopping at the ball, as many people do. As for getting in a little outside practice on trap shots, why not find a sandy area, perhaps an uncrowded beach, where you can simulate bunker situations?

But I believe the biggest handicap in bunker play for the average golfer is mental. Once you prove to yourself that you can come out of sand, you'll relax more and the shot will become almost automatic.

SIMPLIFYING the TRAP SHOT

THE SAND BLAST IS THE EASIEST SHOT OF ALL, DUE TO THE FACT THAT IT IS THE ONLY ONE THAT DOESN'T REQUIRE HITTING THE BALL.

THE CLUBHEAD STRIKES SAND *BEHIND* THE BALL, CREATING PRESSURE WHICH FORCES BOTH BALL AND SAND UP AND OUT.

TO SIMPLIFY BUNKER SHOTS CONCENTRATE ON HITTING AN **AREA**, NOT THE BALL.

ENVISION AN AREA ABOUT **8** INCHES LONG BY **3** INCHES WIDE OF WHICH THE BALL IS A PART.

REMOVE THIS AREA FROM THE TRAP AND YOU ALSO REMOVE THE BALL.

94

The SAND SHOT

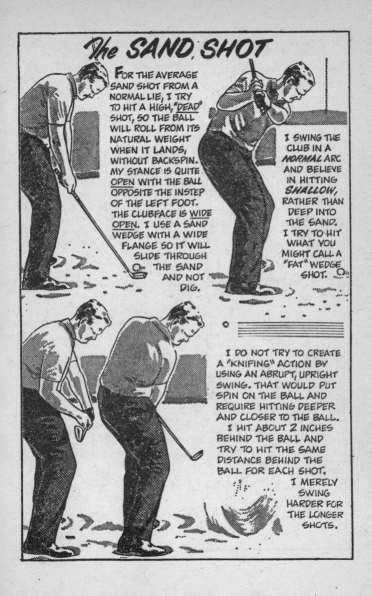

FOR THE AVERAGE SAND SHOT FROM A NORMAL LIE, I TRY TO HIT A HIGH, "DEAD" SHOT, SO THE BALL WILL ROLL FROM ITS NATURAL WEIGHT WHEN IT LANDS, WITHOUT BACKSPIN. MY STANCE IS QUITE OPEN WITH THE BALL OPPOSITE THE INSTEP OF THE LEFT FOOT. THE CLUBFACE IS WIDE OPEN. I USE A SAND WEDGE WITH A WIDE FLANGE SO IT WILL SLIDE THROUGH THE SAND AND NOT DIG.

I SWING THE CLUB IN A *NORMAL* ARC AND BELIEVE IN HITTING *SHALLOW*, RATHER THAN DEEP INTO THE SAND. I TRY TO HIT WHAT YOU MIGHT CALL A "FAT" WEDGE SHOT.

I DO NOT TRY TO CREATE A "KNIFING" ACTION BY USING AN ABRUPT, UPRIGHT SWING. THAT WOULD PUT SPIN ON THE BALL AND REQUIRE HITTING DEEPER AND CLOSER TO THE BALL.

I HIT ABOUT 2 INCHES BEHIND THE BALL AND TRY TO HIT THE SAME DISTANCE BEHIND THE BALL FOR EACH SHOT.

I MERELY SWING HARDER FOR THE LONGER SHOTS.

The LONG DISTANCE BLAST

A BAD LIE IN A FAIRWAY TRAP A GOOD DISTANCE FROM THE GREEN CREATES NO GREAT DISASTER IF HANDLED CORRECTLY.

FOR A SHOT THAT NORMALLY REQUIRES A 7 IRON, A 5 WILL COVER THE SAME DISTANCE, SINCE YOU MUST HIT, IN EFFECT, A LONG EXPLOSION.

PLANT FEET FIRMLY AND ADDRESS THE BALL IN ITS NORMAL POSITION WITH THE CLUBFACE **OPENED WIDE.** THE SHOT WILL FADE, SO AIM LEFT. THEN TAKE THE CLUB BACK SLIGHTLY **OUTSIDE**, USING A FULL BACK-SWING...

OPEN STANCE

OPEN FACE

..HIT AS CLOSE BEHIND THE BALL AS THE SAND PERMITS. STRIKE HARD WITH THE RIGHT HAND AND KEEP WRISTS FROM ROLLING AT OR JUST AFTER IMPACT.

GAUGING the BLAST

IN DETERMINING HOW **HARD** TO SWING WHEN PLAYING A SAND SHOT, HERE IS A **RULE OF THUMB** THAT I USE AND RECOMMEND.

GENERALLY SPEAKING, YOU CAN GAUGE THE SHOT BY SWINGING **TWICE AS HARD** AS YOU WOULD FOR A FAIRWAY CHIP SHOT OF THE SAME DISTANCE.

40 YDS.

20 YDS.

IN OTHER WORDS, IF YOU HAVE A 20 YD. SAND SHOT, SWING AS HARD AS YOU WOULD FOR A 40 YD. CHIP SHOT FROM THE GRASS. OR, IF YOU HAVE A 30 YD. SAND SHOT, SWING AS HARD AS YOU WOULD FOR A 60 YD. SHOT WITH THE PITCHING WEDGE.

AVOID A 'SLIDER' in SAND

THE BLAST THAT SLIDES OFF TO THE RIGHT USUALLY OCCURS BECAUSE THE CLUBHEAD IS NOT COMPLETELY RELEASED THROUGH THE BALL. IN AN ATTEMPT TO CENTER THE HIT RIGHT AT THE BALL, THE PLAYER **DIGS** AND LOSES ACCELERATION OF THE CLUB AT IMPACT.

NORMAL SHOT

SAND SHOT

FOR A BLAST, I BEGIN TO UNCOCK WRISTS SOONER THAN ON NORMAL SHOTS — ALMOST LIKE HITTING FROM THE TOP. THIS INSURES A SWEEP THRU SAND AND UNDER THE BALL WITH A COMPLETE RELEASE. I TRY TO AVOID A LOT OF 'HIT' ON THESE SHOTS.

PLAYING DIFFERENT SAND TEXTURES

OF THE 3 MAIN TYPES OF SAND—FINE, COARSE AND WET—THE EASIEST TO PLAY IS *WET*.

SAND COMPACTED BY RAIN ALLOWS THE CLUBHEAD TO BOUNCE EASILY AND REQUIRES LITTLE CONCERN ABOUT HOW *DEEP* TO HIT. STRIKING A COUPLE OF INCHES BEHIND THE BALL WILL SUFFICE...

WET SAND

COARSE SAND IS A LITTLE MORE DEMANDING, BUT ITS BOUNCE-PRODUCING BASE STILL MAKES IT RELATIVELY SIMPLE TO PLAY...

COARSE

FINE

FINE, POWDERY SAND IS HARDEST TO PLAY. DUE TO LESSER RESISTANCE, THE EXACT DEPTH TO WHICH THE CLUBHEAD DESCENDS IS OF GREATER CONCERN.

BARRETT TAYLOR

• LOFTING SAND SHOTS •

THE CORRECT WAY TO CLEAR A STEEP BUNKER LIP IS QUITE OPPOSITE TO THE POPULAR CONCEPT OF TAKING A LONG LOW BACKSWING THEN TRYING TO LIFT THE BALL OUT BY SCOOPING IT.

TO MAKE THE BALL RISE AS VERTICALLY AS POSSIBLE, THE SWING MUST ALSO BE VERTICAL IN NATURE. THAT IS, THE CLUB IS PICKED UP VERY ABRUPTLY AND BROUGHT DOWN VERY SHARPLY BEHIND THE BALL.

OPEN THE CLUB-FACE AT ADDRESS TO ADD LOFT. THIS PRODUCES A FADING TENDENCY, SO AIM LEFT.

(THIS SAME TECHNIQUE APPLIES TO STEEP BUNKERS IN THE FAIRWAY)

100

CHOKE DOWN IN SAND

●

ONE OF THE BASIC RULES OF BUNKER PLAY IS TO ESTABLISH A FIRM STANCE BY DIGGING THE FEET WELL INTO THE SAND.

THIS PLACES THE HANDS CLOSER TO THE BALL AND REQUIRES THAT YOU COMPENSATE BY GRIPPING FARTHER DOWN THE CLUB SHAFT.

SINCE DISTANCE IS CONTROLLED MORE BY HOW DEEPLY BENEATH THE BALL YOU HIT THAN BY HOW HARD YOU HIT, THE LENGTH OF THE SHOT DETERMINES HOW FAR DOWN TO GRIP THE CLUB.

ON A LONG BLAST WHERE THE NEED IS TO TAKE A MINIMUM OF SAND CHOKE DOWN FARTHER THAN ON AN ORDINARY SHORT SHOT.

STEEP & BURIED? PLAY SAFE!

THERE IS NO SURE-FIRE SYSTEM OF RECOVERY WHEN THE BALL IS BURIED IN THE FACE OF A STEEP BUNKER, BUT YOU CAN SAVE STROKES IF YOU MAKE JUST GETTING OUT YOUR MAIN OBJECTIVE.

THIS MAY REQUIRE AIMING **AWAY** FROM THE PIN TO FIND THE CLEAREST AVENUE OF ESCAPE.

THE LIE WILL CUT DISTANCE, AND IF THE PIN IS **30 FEET** AWAY, AVERAGE GOLFERS WON'T MAKE IT. A SAFE OUT AND LONGER PUTT IS THEREFORE WISE STRATEGY.

SQUARE THE FACE, HIT DOWN AND HOPE IT SLIDES THROUGH SAND TO THE BALL.

STOPPING THE BALL FROM A BURIED LIE

IF MY BALL IS BURIED IN THE SAND AND THE PIN IS CLOSE, LEAVING LITTLE ROOM TO RUN THE BALL, I MUST TRY TO GET THE BALL UP AND STOP IT QUICKLY — A VERY DIFFICULT SHOT.

I WILL PLAY THE BALL FROM A POINT JUST BEHIND THE LEFT HEEL, WITH AN OPEN STANCE AND THE FACE OF THE SAND WEDGE *WIDE OPEN.* I TAKE THE CLUB *STRAIGHT UP* ON THE BACKSWING, THEN TRY TO *HIT DOWN VERY DEEP AND VERY HARD.*

I'M NOT TRYING TO HIT THE BALL I WANT TO GO *UNDER* THE BALL AND POP, OR "SOFT" IT UP.

The BURIED LIE

When the ball lies *BURIED* in a sand trap, I will play it one of two ways; ①—to *RUN* the ball or ②—to *STOP* the ball quickly. First, let me describe my method of hitting so the ball will *RUN* after it lands; when there is plenty of distance between the trap and the pin.

The ball is positioned midway between the feet with a <u>SQUARE</u> stance and a <u>SQUARE</u> clubface. The swing is also relatively <u>SQUARE</u>; that is, I try to swing back and through on a line parallel to the hole. I bring the club down into the sand just behind the ball, and let the ball shoot across the green.

CHAPTER 7

Putting

More than any other part of the golf game, putting brings out the individual in us. It allows for the most experimentation, which is why you see so many contrasting styles of putting, even among the pros on tour.

While there are unorthodox methods which prove successful, I will only concern myself in this section with the conventional techniques that work best for most golfers. There are two cardinal rules you must follow in order to become a good putter: keep your head absolutely still, and make sure the blade of your putter always follows the intended line of the putt. You should also try to incorporate good balance and a firm putting grip into your basic style.

My experience from watching average golfers on the greens is that they tend to baby their putts much more often than they charge the hole. While I don't subscribe to that old cliche, "Never up, never in," I do believe that you must give the ball a chance to drop in. Be firm with your putts. One way of making sure is to keep the blade of the putter moving toward the hole after it has stroked the ball.

As it is with all phases of the game, too much practice can bring negative results. This is especially so with putting, where you are mainly concerned with feel. What I have in the back of my mind when I practice putting is to achieve that fluid, rhythmic feeling between my hands and the way the blade strikes the ball. When I get this feeling with about six or seven balls in a row, I quit—which is the only time you should obey that word in putting.

• The PUTTING GRIP •

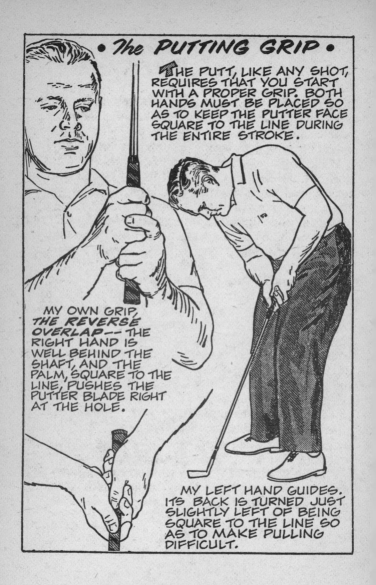

THE PUTT, LIKE ANY SHOT, REQUIRES THAT YOU START WITH A PROPER GRIP. BOTH HANDS MUST BE PLACED SO AS TO KEEP THE PUTTER FACE SQUARE TO THE LINE DURING THE ENTIRE STROKE.

MY OWN GRIP, *THE REVERSE OVERLAP* — THE RIGHT HAND IS WELL BEHIND THE SHAFT, AND THE PALM, SQUARE TO THE LINE, PUSHES THE PUTTER BLADE RIGHT AT THE HOLE.

MY LEFT HAND GUIDES. ITS BACK IS TURNED JUST SLIGHTLY LEFT OF BEING SQUARE TO THE LINE SO AS TO MAKE PULLING DIFFICULT.

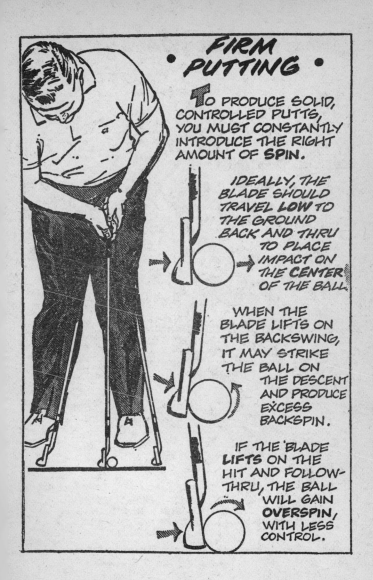

FIRM PUTTING

TO PRODUCE SOLID, CONTROLLED PUTTS, YOU MUST CONSTANTLY INTRODUCE THE RIGHT AMOUNT OF **SPIN**.

IDEALLY, THE BLADE SHOULD TRAVEL **LOW** TO THE GROUND BACK AND THRU TO PLACE IMPACT ON THE **CENTER** OF THE BALL.

WHEN THE BLADE LIFTS ON THE BACKSWING, IT MAY STRIKE THE BALL ON THE DESCENT AND PRODUCE EXCESS BACKSPIN.

IF THE 'BLADE **LIFTS** ON THE HIT AND FOLLOW-THRU, THE BALL WILL GAIN **OVERSPIN**, WITH LESS CONTROL.

FOLLOW THROUGH on PUTTS

THE FOLLOW-THROUGH, NECESSARY FOR TEE AND FAIRWAY SHOTS, IS NO LESS IMPORTANT ON THE GREEN.

IT IS ESPECIALLY IMPORTANT ON SHORT PUTTS, THE FOLLOW-THROUGH COMING MORE NATURALLY ON LONG PUTTS. IT CAN ALSO CURE A LOT OF BACKSWING MISTAKES.

I PERFORM MY FOLLOW-THROUGH BY DRAWING AN IMAGINARY LINE ALONG THE PATH THE BALL WILL TAKE, THEN CONCENTRATING ON CARRYING THE PUTTER FACE ALONG THIS LINE FOR AT LEAST 5 INCHES AFTER THE BALL IS STRUCK.

FOLLOWING THROUGH HELPS TO ASSURE A SOLID ON-LINE PUTT, REGARDLESS OF THE BACKSWING, AND LESSENS THE TENDENCY TO QUIT ON THE SHORT ONES.

The RIGHT ELBOW in PUTTING

THE RIGHT ELBOW PLAYS A KEY ROLE IN PUTTING, SERVING AS A FULCRUM, OR GUIDE, TO HELP STABILIZE THE STROKE.

I FIND THAT HOLDING MY RIGHT ELBOW CLOSE TO MY RIGHT SIDE THROUGHOUT THE STROKE KEEPS THE PUTTER FACE SQUARE AND MOVING STEADILY ON THE LINE OF DIRECTION.

WHEN THE RIGHT ELBOW GETS AWAY FROM THE SIDE, THE PUTTER FACE TENDS TO CLOSE AND TRAVEL OUTSIDE THE DIRECTIONAL LINE AND CAUSE THE PUTT TO BE PULLED.

AVOIDING HEAD MOTION ON PUTTS •

A STEADY HEAD POSITION IS JUST AS VITAL IN PUTTING AS IN ANY OTHER PHASE OF GOLF.

PREMATURE LIFTING OF THE HEAD DURING THE STROKE CAN BE AN UNCONSCIOUS HABIT. OCCASIONALLY MY WIFE, BARBARA, HAS TO POINT THIS OUT TO ME. AFTER FOLLOWING MY ROUND SHE WILL SAY, "YOU'RE MOVING YOUR HEAD AGAIN!" THIS IS A CUE TO SPEND EXTRA CONCENTRATION ON THE MATTER NEXT DAY

ONE THING I DO IS MAKE SURE MY LEFT SHOULDER DOES NOT PULL UP DURING THE STROKE, AS THE HEAD MAY RISE WITH IT.

ANOTHER PRE-CAUTION IS TO WAIT UNTIL THE BALL HAS TRAVELLED 3 OR 4 FEET BEFORE LOOKING UP. IF THIS STILL DOESN'T WORK FOR YOU, TRY NOT TO MOVE YOUR HEAD UNTIL THE BALL STOPS OR DROPS.

• LONG PUTTS •

THREE-PUTT GREENS OFTEN OCCUR BECAUSE OF AN ALL-OUT EFFORT TO SINK THE LONG ONES.

SO, RATHER THAN CHARGE THE CUP ON THESE, I WILL PUTT FOR A SPOT **3** FEET SHORT OF THE HOLE AND TRY TO AVOID GOING MORE THAN **3** FEET PAST THE CUP. THIS GIVES ME A **6**-FOOT CIRCLE IN WHICH TO STOP THE BALL **3** FEET AWAY. WITH A GOOD LINE, SOME WILL DROP ANYWAY.

BARRETT TAYLOR II

3 FT.
3 FT. — 3 FT.
3 FT.

I ALSO STAND MORE *ERECT* THAN ON SHORTER PUTTS. UP HIGH, I FIND I CAN SEE THE HOLE AND THE LINE MORE EASILY.

• THE SHORT PUTT •

EASING UP ON THE STROKE IS THE MOST FREQUENTLY COMMITTED ERROR ON SHORT PUTTS.

THE RESULTING DISMAY AS THE BALL DIES SHORT OF THE HOLE OR SLIDES JUST OFF TO THE SIDE CAN BE AVOIDED IF YOU CONCENTRATE UPON MAKING A *FIRM* STROKE, NOT JUST AT IMPACT, BUT AFTER IMPACT AS WELL.

BARRETT TAYLOR.

AFTER DETERMINING THE LINE OF THE PUTT, I AIM FOR A SPOT JUST SHORT OF THE HOLE OVER WHICH THE BALL MUST TRAVEL. THEN, MAKING SURE MY HEAD AND BODY REMAIN PERFECTLY STILL, I STROKE FIRMLY, CONTINUING WELL THROUGH THE BALL.

PUTTING DOWNHILL

MOST 3-PUTT GREENS FROM ABOVE THE HOLE OCCUR THROUGH A *FEAR*, RATHER THAN AN ACTUALITY, OF THE BALL GOING TOO FAR PAST THE CUP.

THIS CAUSES SOME PLAYERS TO EASE-UP ON THE STROKE AND LEAVE STILL A TRICKY DOWNHILL SECOND.

IT IS MOST IMPORTANT TO GET THE BALL DOWN *TO* THE HOLE—AND THIS REQUIRES A *FIRM*, CONTINUING STROKE. IT DOESN'T HAVE TO BE HARD TO BE FIRM...

...NATURALLY, YOU DON'T WANT TO GO FAR PAST, BUT A 3 FOOT *UP-HILL* PUTT IS MUCH EASIER THAN A 3-FOOT *DOWNHILLER*.

BARRETT TAYLOR

• PUTTING UPHILL •

LEAVING THE BALL SHORT ON AN UPHILL PUTT CONSTITUTES ONE OF GOLF'S CARDINAL SINS. (A POINT, INCIDENTALLY, ON WHICH I AM FAR FROM GUILTLESS.)

THIS IS THE EASIEST OF ALL PUTTS TO MAKE. THE BACK OF THE CUP BEING HIGHER THAN THE FRONT OFFERS, IN EFFECT MORE TARGET THAN NORMAL.

Barrett Taylor

THE STEEP ANGLE PLUS THE RESISTANCE OF GRAVITY ALLOWS THE BALL TO BE STROKED VERY BOLDLY, YET DROP. THEREIN LIES THE RULE FOR PUTTING UPHILL. STROKE FIRMLY AND MAKE SURE THE BALL REACHES THE HOLE. SELDOM WILL IT GO TOO FAR PAST.

UPHILL   LEVEL

PERSPECTIVE VIEW OF UPHILL, PUTT COMPARED WITH THAT OF LEVEL SHOWS ADVANTAGE OF BEING BELOW THE CUP.

114

PUTTING from the FRINGE

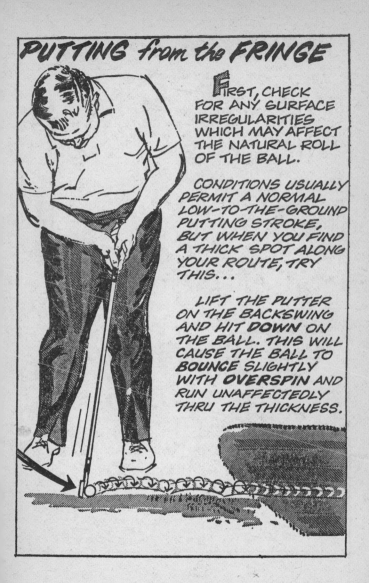

First, check for any surface irregularities which may affect the natural roll of the ball.

Conditions usually permit a normal low-to-the-ground putting stroke, but when you find a thick spot along your route, try this...

Lift the putter on the backswing and hit **down** on the ball. This will cause the ball to **bounce** slightly with **overspin** and run unaffectedly thru the thickness.

PUTTING OUT OF SAND

THIS IS A GOOD PERCENTAGE SHOT PROVIDED THE TRAP IS RELATIVELY FLAT WITH LITTLE OR NO OVERHANGING LIP.

USE YOUR NORMAL PUTTING STYLE BUT HIT THE BALL OFF THE *TOE*, RATHER THAN THE CENTER, OF THE BLADE. THIS TENDS TO GIVE A *SLINGING* ACTION TO THE PUTT, WHICH REDUCES NATURAL BACKSPIN AND PRODUCES MORE CONSISTENT ROLL.

HERE THE PUTTER PROVIDES THE CONTROL A DELICATE EXPLOSION MIGHT NOT.

ON PRACTICING PUTTING

To MY WAY OF THINKING, PRACTICING PUTTING IS GOOD, YET IN CERTAIN RESPECTS, IT IS BAD.

SOME DEGREE OF PRACTICE IS NECESSARY TO DEVELOP A CORRECT *STROKE*—THIS IS IMPORTANT—BUT IN TRYING TO LEARN TO CONTROL THE *SPEED* OF THE PUTT, IT CAN BE HARMFUL TO PRACTICE TOO EXTENSIVELY ON ANY ONE TYPE OF GREEN.

SPEED OF GREENS VARY FROM COURSE TO COURSE—EVEN FROM HOLE TO HOLE—AND ALTHOUGH YOU MAY MASTER SPEED CONTROL ON ONE TYPE OF GREEN, YOU WILL HAVE TO CHANGE THINGS ALL AROUND FOR THE NEXT ONE.

THEREFORE, I PRACTICE MY PUTTING ONLY ON THE COURSE THAT I'M GOING TO PLAY, AND THEN VERY LITTLE — JUST ENOUGH TO GET THE "FEEL."

THE *STROKE* IS THE MAIN THING —AND IF MINE FALTERS, I TAKE TIME OFF AND WORK TO GET IT BACK. ONCE REGAINED, I AVOID OVERPRACTICE.

PUTTING IS A THING OF *FEEL*, NOT SOMETHING "AUTOMATIC."

CHAPTER 8

Quick Cures

It's frustrating to start a round of golf full of confidence and then to discover you are doing something wrong that is drastically affecting your score. Often, moments like this make you do desperate things, and before you know it, you can't do anything right.

The best way to correct this, of course, is to consult your professional the next chance you get. But in the midst of a round, this is not practical advice. You want immediate help, even if it's only enough to get you to the 18th hole. In this final section, I've singled out a few of the more common errors that crop up among high-handicap players and supplied some of my own instant remedies for them. It might be a good idea to carry this book in your golf bag and to pull it out when some bug develops in your game.

I don't deal with the slice *per se* here, even though this is one of the most frequent afflictions of average golfers. But slicing is mostly a chronic fault that cannot be corrected simply in one lesson or two; it is symptomatic of perhaps several things you are doing wrong. The essential checkpoints of slicing are to see if you are making your arc outside the intended line of flight, and if you are taking an open stance. If you will at least hit from a closed stance and swing-out, you've got a fighting chance of straightening out that slice. But you should let your pro see your swing to keep it in the proper groove.

If you treat a golf problem as you would a toothache, take care of it early, before it develops into something worse, your game will improve. And that's the best way to play golf.

How to AVOID HITTING from the TOP

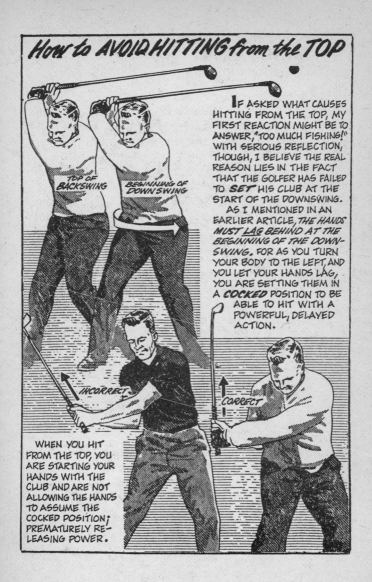

TOP OF BACKSWING

BEGINNING OF DOWNSWING

IF ASKED WHAT CAUSES HITTING FROM THE TOP, MY FIRST REACTION MIGHT BE TO ANSWER, "TOO MUCH FISHING!" WITH SERIOUS REFLECTION, THOUGH, I BELIEVE THE REAL REASON LIES IN THE FACT THAT THE GOLFER HAS FAILED TO *SET* HIS CLUB AT THE START OF THE DOWNSWING.

AS I MENTIONED IN AN EARLIER ARTICLE, *THE HANDS MUST LAG BEHIND AT THE BEGINNING OF THE DOWN-SWING.* FOR AS YOU TURN YOUR BODY TO THE LEFT, AND YOU LET YOUR HANDS LAG, YOU ARE SETTING THEM IN A *COCKED* POSITION TO BE ABLE TO HIT WITH A POWERFUL, DELAYED ACTION.

INCORRECT

CORRECT

WHEN YOU HIT FROM THE TOP, YOU ARE STARTING YOUR HANDS WITH THE CLUB AND ARE NOT ALLOWING THE HANDS TO ASSUME THE COCKED POSITION; PREMATURELY RE-LEASING POWER.

AVOIDING SKIED SHOTS

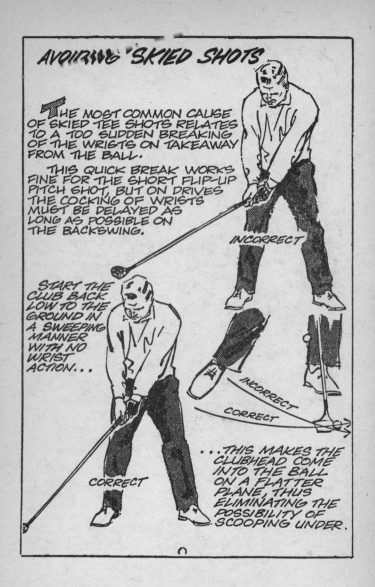

THE MOST COMMON CAUSE OF SKIED TEE SHOTS RELATES TO A TOO SUDDEN BREAKING OF THE WRISTS ON TAKEAWAY FROM THE BALL.

THIS QUICK BREAK WORKS FINE FOR THE SHORT FLIP-UP PITCH SHOT, BUT ON DRIVES THE COCKING OF WRISTS MUST BE DELAYED AS LONG AS POSSIBLE ON THE BACKSWING.

INCORRECT

START THE CLUB BACK LOW TO THE GROUND IN A SWEEPING MANNER WITH NO WRIST ACTION...

INCORRECT

CORRECT

CORRECT

...THIS MAKES THE CLUBHEAD COME INTO THE BALL ON A FLATTER PLANE, THUS ELIMINATING THE POSSIBILITY OF SCOOPING UNDER.

The PULL-HOOK
A CAUSE and A CURE —

THE DREADED PULL-HOOK IS GENERALLY INITIATED BY INSUFFICIENT **SHOULDER-TURN** ON THE BACKSWING, WHICH IN TURN CAUSES THE SHOULDERS TO LEAD THE DOWNSWING. THE RIGHT SHOULDER IS PULLED OUT AND OVER FOR THE HIT AND THE BALL WINDS UP IN LEFT FIELD.

THE FIRST STEP TOWARD CORRECTION IS TO MAKE SURE YOU TAKE A FULL SHOULDER-TURN...

...THEN, IN STARTING THE DOWNSWING, MAKE THE FIRST MOVE WITH YOUR **HIPS** AND **LEGS**, LETTING THE SHOULDERS LAG BEHIND. THIS WILL KEEP THE SHOULDERS IN THE CORRECT PLANE AND BEHIND THE SHOT.

PREVENTING AN OUTSIDE LOOP

A REROUTING OF THE CLUB TO THE OUTSIDE OF ITS PROPER ARC CAN USUALLY BE TRACED TO BODY SWAY.

WHEN A PLAYER MOVES HIS HIPS LATERALLY ON THE BACKSWING, INSTEAD OF JUST TURNING THEM, HE TENDS TO SPIN ON HIS RIGHT HIP AS THE DOWNSWING STARTS, FAILS TO RETURN HIS WEIGHT TO THE LEFT AND, THUS, CREATES AN OUTSIDE LOOP.

INCORRECT

INCORRECT

CORRECT

CORRECT

YOU'LL FIND IT PRETTY HARD TO LOOP OUTSIDE IF YOU STRIVE TO MERELY *TURN* THE HIPS GOING BACK, THEN *SLIDE* AS WELL AS TURN THEM COMING DOWN.

AVOIDING A SHANK

THERE ARE ANY NUMBER OF ERRORS WHICH CAN CAUSE THE HOSEL OF THE CLUB TO STRIKE THE BALL AND PRODUCE WHAT IS KNOWN AS A SHANKED SHOT.

A PLAYER MAY RELEASE FROM THE TOP; HE MAY MOVE HIPS TOO FAR FORWARD AND GO OVER THE BALL; HE MAY SPIN ON HIS RIGHT SIDE; OR HE MAY 'BELLY' THE BALL BY SWINGING TOO MUCH FROM THE INSIDE.

THE UNDERLYING CAUSE, HOWEVER, IS HEAD MOTION. FOR IF YOU LINE UP AT A REASONABLE DISTANCE FROM THE BALL AND KEEP YOUR HEAD IN A STATIONARY POSITION ALL DURING THE SWING, A SHANK WILL RARELY OCCUR

FALLING BACKWARD?

THIS OFTEN OCCURS WHEN THE DOWNSWING IS TOO FAST TO ALLOW SUFFICIENT TRANSFER OF WEIGHT TO THE LEFT FOOT.

THE HIPS ARE UNABLE TO LEAD AND MOST OF THE WEIGHT REMAINS ON THE **RIGHT** FOOT AND THE REST FALLS ONTO THE **HEEL** OF THE **LEFT** FOOT.

PROPER WEIGHT SHIFT DEPENDS ON PROPER SWING TEMPO. TIME YOUR SWING SMOOTHLY AND YOU WILL BE ABLE TO GET WEIGHT TO THE CENTER OF THE LEFT FOOT WHERE IT BELONGS

BARRETT TAYLOR

FALLING FORWARD ?

THIS USUALLY COMES FROM SHIFTING WEIGHT TOO QUICKLY ON THE DOWN-SWING. SHOULDERS, RATHER THAN HIPS, LEAD AND WEIGHT WINDS UP ON THE **TOE** OF THE LEFT FOOT.

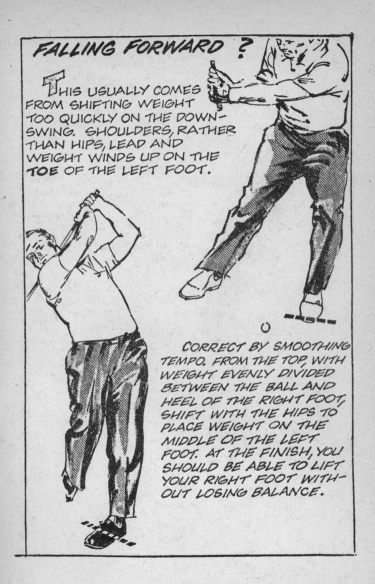

CORRECT BY SMOOTHING TEMPO, FROM THE TOP, WITH WEIGHT EVENLY DIVIDED BETWEEN THE BALL AND HEEL OF THE RIGHT FOOT, SHIFT WITH THE HIPS TO PLACE WEIGHT ON THE MIDDLE OF THE LEFT FOOT. AT THE FINISH, YOU SHOULD BE ABLE TO LIFT YOUR RIGHT FOOT WITH-OUT LOSING BALANCE.

STAYING WITH the SHOT

ONE HELPFUL WAY TO SOLVE THE *HARD-TO-CURE* PROBLEM OF PULLING UP, OR COMING OFF THE BALL IS TO FIND A PRACTICE TEE, THEN MAKE AN EXAGGERATED EFFORT TO KEEP YOUR HEAD FROM COMING UP AFTER THE HIT.

MY METHOD IS TO TRY TO COMPLETELY FINISH THE SWING WITHOUT LIFTING MY HEAD OR TAKING MY EYES OFF THE ORIGINAL BALL LOCATION.

WHEN YOU RESUME YOUR NORMAL SWING AFTER THIS TYPE OF SESSION, YOU WILL FIND THAT YOUR HEAD AND BODY TEND TO HOLD POSITION ALMOST AUTOMATICALLY. NOT UNTIL WELL AFTER IMPACT WILL THE HEAD RISE.

CHECKPOINTS for PRACTICE

I HAVE SEVERAL THINGS IN MY SWING THAT I HAVE TO WATCH OUT FOR—AS I'M SURE EVERYONE HAS IN HIS OWN—AND IF I'M PLAYING BADLY, I HAVE CERTAIN *CHECKPOINTS* TO CONCENTRATE UPON DURING PRACTICE.

I CHECK TO MAKE SURE THAT MY BACKSWING IS *SLOW,* THAT THE WEIGHT IS ON THE *INSIDE* OF THE RIGHT FOOT, AND THAT THE RIGHT ELBOW IS BASICALLY *CLOSE* TO MY BODY.

I ALSO WANT TO BE SURE THAT I'M SHIFTING MY WEIGHT PROPERLY AND THAT MY POSITION THROUGH THE HITTING AREA IS CORRECT.

I PRACTICE EACH SEGMENT OF THE SWING INDIVIDUALLY AND TRY TO REGAIN THE PROPER FEEL. I DON'T CARE WHERE THE BALL GOES FOR A WHILE. AFTER I HAVE MOLDED ALL THESE THINGS TOGETHER, AND EVERYTHING IS IN ITS PROPER PLACE, THEN I WORK TOWARD HITTING THE BALL. I FEEL THAT THIS IS THE BEST WAY TO PRACTICE AND SUGGEST YOU TRY IT THE NEXT TIME YOUR SWING FALTERS.

THINK TWICE BEFORE MAKING CHANGES

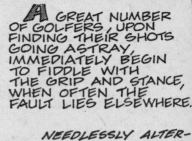

A GREAT NUMBER OF GOLFERS, UPON FINDING THEIR SHOTS GOING ASTRAY, IMMEDIATELY BEGIN TO FIDDLE WITH THE GRIP AND STANCE, WHEN OFTEN THE FAULT LIES ELSEWHERE.

NEEDLESSLY ALTERING A SOUND GRIP IS LIKE TRYING TO CORRECT A FAULT WITH A FAULT. LOCATE THE TROUBLE BEFORE YOU ADJUST.

BEGIN YOUR SWING CHECK WITH THE BASICS. IF YOU FIND THE GRIP AND STANCE IN ORDER, CHECK YOUR BACKSWING, HEAD POSITION, FOOT ACTION, WEIGHT SHIFT, ETC.

REMEMBER, TOO MANY EXPERIMENTAL CHANGES WILL OFTEN DESTROY THE GOOD IN A SWING AND MAKE FOR BAD GOLF.